GLOBALVIEWPOINTS

Geoengineering: Counteracting Climate Change

Other Books in the Global Viewpoints Series

GLOBALVIEWPOINTS

Geoengineering: Counteracting Climate Change

Rita Santos, Book Editor

GREENHAVEN
PUBLISHING

Published in 2019 by Greenhaven Publishing, LLC
353 3rd Avenue, Suite 255, New York, NY 10010

First Edition

Articles in Greenhaven Publishing anthologies are often edited for length to meet page
requirements. In addition, original titles of these works are changed to clearly present
the main thesis and to explicitly indicate the author's opinion. Every effort is made to
ensure that Greenhaven Publishing accurately reflects the original intent of the authors.
Every effort has been made to trace the owners of the copyrighted material.

Cover image: VICTOR HABBICK VISIONS/SCIENCE PHOTO LIBRARY/Getty Images

Cataloging-in Publication Data

Names: Santos, Rita, editor.
Title: Geoengineering: counteracting climate change / edited by Rita Santos.
Description: New York : Greenhaven Publishing, 2019. | Series: Global viewpoints |
  Includes bibliographical references and index. | Audience: Grades 9-12.
Identifiers: LCCN ISBN 9781534503465 (library bound) | ISBN 9781534503472 (pbk.)
Subjects: LCSH: Environmental engineering--Juvenile literature. | Climate change
  mitigation--Juvenile literature. | Climatic changes--Juvenile literature.
Classification: LCC TA170.G464 2019 | DDC 628--dc23

Manufactured in the United States of America

Website: http://greenhavenpublishing.com

Contents

Chapter 2: Current Geoengineering Theories

Chapter 3: Why a Global Effort Is Needed

Chapter 4: Looking to the Future

Foreword

"The problems of all of humanity can only be solved by all of humanity."
—Swiss author Friedrich Dürrenmatt

Global interdependence has become an undeniable reality. Mass media and technology have increased worldwide access to information and created a society of global citizens. Understanding and navigating this global community is a challenge, requiring a high degree of information literacy and a new level of learning sophistication.

Building on the success of its flagship series, Opposing Viewpoints, Greenhaven Publishing has created the Global Viewpoints series to examine a broad range of current, often controversial topics of worldwide importance from a variety of international perspectives. Providing students and other readers with the information they need to explore global connections and think critically about worldwide implications, each Global Viewpoints volume offers a panoramic view of a topic of widespread significance.

Drugs, famine, immigration—a broad, international treatment is essential to do justice to social, environmental, health, and political issues such as these. Junior high, high school, and early college students, as well as general readers, can all use Global Viewpoints anthologies to discern the complexities relating to each issue. Readers will be able to examine unique national perspectives while, at the same time, appreciating the interconnectedness that global priorities bring to all nations and cultures.

Material in each volume is selected from a diverse range of sources, including journals, magazines, newspapers, nonfiction books, speeches, government documents, pamphlets, organization newsletters, and position papers. Global Viewpoints is truly global, with material drawn primarily from international sources available in English and secondarily from US sources with extensive international coverage.

Features of each volume in the Global Viewpoints series include:

- An **annotated table of contents** that provides a brief summary of each essay in the volume, including the name of the country or area covered in the essay.

- An **introduction** specific to the volume topic.

- A **world map** to help readers locate the countries or areas covered in the essays.

- For each viewpoint, an **introduction** that contains notes about the author and source of the viewpoint explains why material from the specific country is being presented, summarizes the main points of the viewpoint, and offers three **guided reading questions** to aid in understanding and comprehension.

- **For further discussion questions** that promote critical thinking by asking the reader to compare and contrast aspects of the viewpoints or draw conclusions about perspectives and arguments.

- A worldwide list of **organizations to contact** for readers seeking additional information.

- A **periodical bibliography** for each chapter and a **bibliography of books** on the volume topic to aid in further research.

- A comprehensive **subject index** to offer access to people, places, events, and subjects cited in the text.

Global Viewpoints is designed for a broad spectrum of readers who want to learn more about current events, history, political science, government, international relations, economics, environmental science, world cultures, and sociology—students doing research for class assignments or debates, teachers and faculty seeking to supplement course materials, and others wanting to understand current issues better. By presenting how people in various countries perceive the root causes, current consequences, and proposed solutions to worldwide challenges, Global Viewpoints volumes offer readers opportunities to enhance their global awareness and their knowledge of cultures worldwide.

Introduction

> *"Few serious scientists would argue that we should begin deploying geoengineering anytime soon. But with time running out, it's imperative to explore any option that could pull the world back from the brink of catastrophe."*
> *"The Growing Case for Geoengineering," by James Temple, MIT Technology Review*

The question of whether or not climate change is occurring has been answered, for those who want to listen. There is now scientific consensus that not only does global warming exist, but humans are the primary cause of it. The next question for scientists is, of course, what can be done to stabilize our climate.

Most scientists agree that climate mitigation, such as making efforts to reduce greenhouse gas emissions and discontinue the use of fossil fuels, is necessary to halt climate change. But some don't think mitigation will be enough to negate the effects of climate change. Some believe that we must also be working to undo the damage that's been done to the atmosphere through centuries of burning fossil fuels and production of other greenhouse gases. Scientists and engineers all over the world have already begun to explore ways to alter the Earth's climate. This new field of study is referred to as climate engineering, or geoengineering.

Geoengineering refers to the deliberate altering of the Earth's climate. The two current models of geoengineering are greenhouse gas removal and solar radiation management. The field of geoengineering is in its infancy and is still years away from large-scale testing. There is legitimate concern in the scientific community that geoengineering efforts could cause unforeseen problems, like cooling the Earth too much or causing excessive rainfall. But no matter what the outcome, geoengineering could potentially affect all life on the planet. Scientists must proceed with caution so that they don't further harm the climate.

The entire planet is feeling the effects of global warming, but the effects are different in each nation. Some countries, like Russia and Canada, could benefit from warmer temperatures, but rising temperatures become deadly heat waves in countries like India. This uneven distribution of the negative effects of global warming has allowed some countries to ignore the seriousness of global warming for years. But that time is slowly coming to an end.

The Earth's climate doesn't care about the national boundaries drawn by humans. Stabilizing the climate will require the cooperation of the whole world. This is why the Paris Agreement, an international agreement to lower greenhouse gas emissions, was agreed to by the participating 196 countries at the 2015 United Nations Climate Change Conference.

While the United States would later become the only country to leave the agreement, it was still a positive step forward in the fight against climate change. The Paris Agreement allows each nation to create its own plan toward fighting climate change. While some countries are wary of funding experimental and risky geoengineering theories, other countries lack these hesitations.

Geoengineering offers scientists a unique ethical quandary. Whether the effects of the technology are positive or negative, they will impact all life on Earth. As it is impossible to get the consent of every human, how can the scientific community determine what risks are worth taking? And how can they get their message across when their cause is so often hijacked and corrupted by politicians? As the effects of climate change become increasingly deadlier, will people's feelings about the need for geoengineering change? As with any new scientific field, there are still many questions left to answer. Shining a light on this fascinating subject, the viewpoints in *Global Viewpoints: Geoengineering: Counteracting Climate Change* examine and explore the complex undertaking of saving the planet.

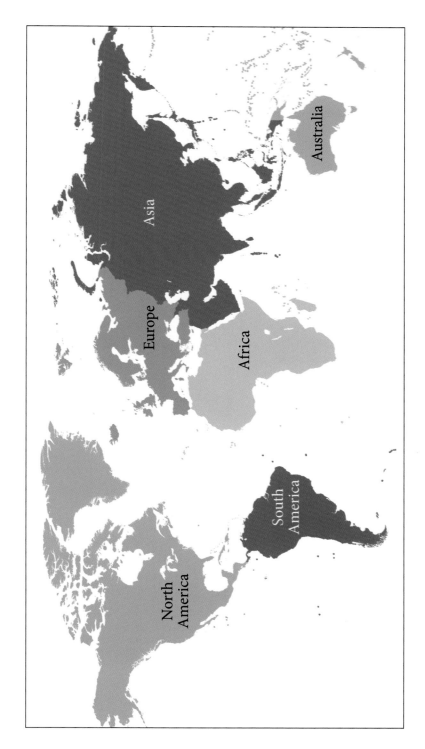

GLOBAL VIEWPOINTS

CHAPTER 1

Stopping Climate Change

What Is Climate Change?

Enviropedia

While climate change is a term used constantly in the media, it is rarely clearly defined. Enviropedia is an educational website focusing on the atmospheric environment that hopes to clear up some of the mysteries surrounding environmental issues. Its goal is to educate the public on issues surrounding air pollution and climate change. Here it provides a brief overview of some of the natural and human-made causes of climate change. It explains how palaeoclimatology, the study of the history of Earth's climate change, hopes to provide a clearer picture of how humans are affecting the delicate balance of Earth's climate.

As you read, consider the following questions:

1. What is climate?
2. What can palaeoclimatology tell us about Earth?
3. What impact are humans having on climate change?

Climate is the long-term statistical expression of short-term weather. Climate can be defined as "expected weather." When changes in the expected weather occur, we call these climate changes. They can be defined by the differences between average weather conditions at two separate times. Climate may change in different ways, over different time scales and at different geographical scales. In recent times, scientists have become interested in global

"Introduction to Climate Change," Enviropedia.

warming, due to mankind's impact on the climate system, through the enhancement of the natural greenhouse effect.

The overall state of the global climate is determined by the amount of energy stored by the climate system, and in particular the balance between energy the Earth receives from the Sun and the energy which the Earth releases back to space, called the global energy balance. How this energy balance is regulated depends upon the flows of energy within the global climate system. Major causes of climate change involve any process that can alter the global energy balance, and the energy flows within the climate system. Causes of climate change include changes in the Earth's orbit around the Sun, changes in the amount of energy coming from the Sun, changes in ocean circulation or changes in the composition of the atmosphere. Large volcanic eruptions can affect the global climate over only a few years. By contrast, the movement of continents around the world over hundreds of millions of years can also affect global climate, but only over these much longer time scales.

Throughout the Earth's history climate has fluctuated between periods of relative warmth and relative cold. Palaeoclimatology is the study of climate and climate change prior to the period of direct measurements. Direct records of temperature and other climatic elements span only a tiny fraction of the Earth's climatic history, and so provide an inadequate perspective on climatic change and the evolution of the climate today and in the future. A longer perspective on climate variability can be obtained by the study of natural phenomena which are climate-dependent. Such phenomena provide a record of past climates, and are revealed through the study of, amongst other techniques, tree rings, ice cores and sea floor sediments.

In the last 100 years or so, the Earth's surface and lowest part of the atmosphere have warmed up on average by about $0.6\,^{\circ}$C. During this period, the amount of greenhouse gases in the atmosphere has increased, largely as a result of the burning of fossil fuels for energy and transportation, and land use changes, for food by mankind. In the last 20 years, concern has grown that these two phenomena are, at least in part, associated with each other. That is to say, global warming is now considered most probably to be due to the man-made increases in greenhouse gas emissions. Whilst other natural causes of climate change, including changes in the amount of energy coming from the Sun and shifting patterns of ocean circulation, can cause global climate to change over similar periods of time, the balance of evidence now indicates that there is a discernible human influence on the global climate.

How NASA Defines and Studies Climate Change

Dan Stillman and Denise Miller

NASA may be most famous for putting a man on the moon, but it's also at the forefront of Earth's climate change research. The Earth Observing System (EOS) uses satellites to monitor Earth's land surface, oceans, atmosphere, and biosphere, which is composed of all of Earth's different ecosystems. The EOS gives scientists the ability to track how Earth's climate is changing. NASA currently supports the global opinion that Earth's temperature is rising dangerously and that climate change is mostly human-made. This viewpoint offers a brief introduction to what climate change is and how it's being monitored by NASA. Stillman is with the Institute for Global Environmental Strategies. Miller is with NASA Educational Technology Services.

As you read, consider the following questions:

1. What do scientists mean by the phrase "climate change"?
2. What are some natural causes of climate change, as mentioned in the viewpoint?
3. What are greenhouse gases?

The climate of a region or city is its typical or average weather. For example, the climate of Hawaii is sunny and warm. But the climate of Antarctica is freezing cold. Earth's climate is the average of all the world's regional climates.

"What Are Climate and Climate Change?" by Sandra May, National Aeronautics and Space Administration, August 4, 2017. Reprinted by permission.

Climate change, therefore, is a change in the typical or average weather of a region or city. This could be a change in a region's average annual rainfall, for example. Or it could be a change in a city's average temperature for a given month or season.

Climate change is also a change in Earth's overall climate. This could be a change in Earth's average temperature, for example. Or it could be a change in Earth's typical precipitation patterns.

What Is the Difference Between Weather and Climate?

Weather is the short-term changes we see in temperature, clouds, precipitation, humidity and wind in a region or a city. Weather can vary greatly from one day to the next, or even within the same day. In the morning the weather may be cloudy and cool. But by afternoon it may be sunny and warm.

The climate of a region or city is its weather averaged over many years. This is usually different for different seasons. For example, a region or city may tend to be warm and humid during summer. But it may tend to be cold and snowy during winter.

The climate of a city, region or the entire planet changes very slowly. These changes take place on the scale of tens, hundreds and thousands of years.

Is Earth's Climate Changing?

Earth's climate is always changing. In the past, Earth's climate has gone through warmer and cooler periods, each lasting thousands of years.

Observations show that Earth's climate has been warming. Its average temperature has risen a little more than one degree Fahrenheit during the past 100 years or so. This amount may not seem like much. But small changes in Earth's average temperature can lead to big impacts.

What Is Causing Earth's Climate to Change?

Some causes of climate change are natural. These include changes in Earth's orbit and in the amount of energy coming from the sun. Ocean changes and volcanic eruptions are also natural causes of climate change.

Most scientists think that recent warming can't be explained by nature alone. Most scientists say it's very likely that most of the warming since the mid-1900s is due to the burning of coal, oil and gas. Burning these fuels is how we produce most of the energy that we use every day. This burning adds heat-trapping gases, such as carbon dioxide, into the air. These gases are called greenhouse gases.

What Is the Forecast for Earth's Climate?

Scientists use climate models to predict how Earth's climate will change. Climate models are computer programs with mathematical equations. They are programmed to simulate past climate as accurately as possible. This gives scientists some confidence in a climate model's ability to predict the future.

Climate models predict that Earth's average temperature will keep rising over the next 100 years or so. There may be a year or years where Earth's average temperature is steady or even falls. But the overall trend is expected to be up.

Earth's average temperature is expected to rise even if the amount of greenhouse gases in the atmosphere decreases. But the rise would be less than if greenhouse gas amounts remain the same or increase.

What Is the Impact of Earth's Warming Climate?

Some impacts already are occurring. For example, sea levels are rising, and snow and ice cover is decreasing. Rainfall patterns and growing seasons are changing. Further sea-level rise and melting of snow and ice are likely as Earth warms. The warming climate likely will cause more floods, droughts and heat waves. The heat waves may get hotter, and hurricanes may get stronger.

What Is the Difference Between "Climate Change" and "Global Warming"?

"Global warming" refers to the long-term increase in Earth's average temperature. "Climate change" refers to any long-term change in Earth's climate, or in the climate of a region or city. This includes warming, cooling and changes besides temperature.

How Does NASA Study Climate Change?

Some NASA satellites and instruments observe Earth's land, air, water and ice. Others monitor the sun and the amount of energy coming from it. Together, these observations are important for knowing the past and present state of Earth's climate. They are important for understanding how Earth's climate works. And they are important for predicting future climate change.

What Is Being Done About Climate Change?

The United States and other countries are taking steps to limit or reduce greenhouse gases in the atmosphere. These steps include using energy more efficiently and using more clean energy. Clean energy is energy that puts less or no greenhouse gases into the atmosphere. The sun, wind and water are sources of clean energy.

Many nations, states and communities are planning for climate change impacts that may be unavoidable. For example, some coastal areas are planning for flooding and land loss that may result from rising sea levels.

What Can You Do to Help?

You can help by using less energy and water. For example, turn off lights and TVs when you leave a room. And turn off the water when brushing your teeth. You can help by planting trees, which absorb carbon dioxide from the atmosphere.

Another way to help is by learning about Earth and its climate. The more you know about how Earth's climate works, the more you'll be able to help solve problems related to climate change.

Climate Change Threatens Crop Yield

Department for Business, Energy & Industrial Strategy

In the following viewpoint, the UK's Department for Business, Energy & Industrial Strategy argues that climate change is happening now, and it's in part caused by human activity. When it comes to climate change, the media tends to report mostly on the effects of rising temperature and rising tides, but there are other devastating effects to consider. Climate change also affects rainfall patterns around the world. While some regions experience severe droughts, others have so much rain that floods become more common. These types of weather disruptions affect food crops around the world. Can geoengineering provide solutions to climate change before a global "tipping point" is reached? For researchers at the Department for Business, Energy & Industrial Strategy, the answer is clear; everyone must work together to prevent the most harmful effects of climate change. The Department for Business, Energy & Industrial Strategy is a government department of the UK responsible for climate change policy and science and innovation.

As you read, consider the following questions:

1. What are some other effects of climate change besides rising temperatures?
2. What effects will climate change have on humans?
3. How will climate change affect the food supply?

"Climate change explained," Department for Business, Energy & Industrial Strategy, Crown copyright, October 23, 2014.

Climate change is happening and is due to human activity, this includes global warming and greater risk of flooding, droughts and heat waves.

Climate Change Now

There is clear evidence to show that climate change is happening. Measurements show that the average temperature at the Earth's surface has risen by about 0.8°C over the last century. 13 of the 14 warmest years on record have occurred in the 21st century and in the last 30 years each decade has been hotter than the previous one. This change in temperature hasn't been the same everywhere; the increase has been greater over land than over the oceans and has been particularly fast in the Arctic.

The UK is already affected by rising temperatures. The average temperature in Britain is now 1°C higher than it was 100 years ago and 0.5°C higher than it was in the 1970s.

Although it is clear that the climate is warming in the long-term, note that temperatures aren't expected to rise every single year. Natural fluctuations will still cause unusually cold years and seasons.

Along with warming at the Earth's surface, many other changes in the climate are occurring:

- warming oceans
- melting polar ice and glaciers
- rising sea levels
- more extreme weather events

Warming Oceans

While the temperature rise at the Earth's surface may get the most headlines, the temperature of the oceans has been increasing too. This warming has been measured all the way down to 2 km deep.

The chemistry of the oceans is also changing as they absorb much of the excess carbon dioxide being emitted into the atmosphere. This is causing the oceans to become acidic more rapidly than at any point in the last 65 million years.

Melting Polar Ice and Glaciers
As the Arctic warms, sea ice is decreasing rapidly. In the Antarctic, sea ice has slowly increased, driven by local changes in wind patterns and freshening sea water. Over the past 20 years the ice sheets (the great masses of land ice at the poles) in Greenland and the Antarctic have shrunk, as have most glaciers around the world.

Rising Sea Levels
As land ice melts and the warming oceans expand, sea levels have risen. Between 1901 and 2010 the global average sea level rose by 0.19 metres, likely faster than at any point in the last 2,000 years.

More Extreme Weather Events
More damaging extreme weather events are being seen around the world. Heat waves have become more frequent and are lasting longer. The height of extreme sea levels caused by storms has increased. Warming is expected to cause more intense, heavy rainfall events. In North America and Europe, where long-term rainfall measurements exist, this change has already been observed.

Causes of Climate Change
Rising levels of carbon dioxide and other gases, such as methane, in the atmosphere create a "greenhouse effect," trapping the Sun's energy and causing the Earth, and in particular the oceans, to warm. Heating of the oceans accounts for over nine tenths of the trapped energy. Scientists have known about this greenhouse effect since the 19th century.

The higher the amounts of greenhouse gases in the atmosphere, the warmer the Earth becomes. Recent climate change is happening largely as a result of this warming, with smaller contributions from natural influences like variations in the Sun's output.

Carbon dioxide levels have increased by more than 40% since before the industrial revolution. Other greenhouse gases have increased by similarly large amounts. All the evidence shows that this increase in greenhouse gases is almost entirely due to human activity. The increase is mainly caused by:

- burning of fossil fuels for energy
- agriculture and deforestation
- the manufacture of cement, chemicals and metals

About 43% of the carbon dioxide produced goes into the atmosphere, and the rest is absorbed by plants and the oceans. Deforestation reduces the number of trees absorbing carbon dioxide and releases the carbon contained in those trees.

Evidence and Analysis

Evidence from Past Climate Change
Ancient ice from the polar ice sheets reveal natural temperature changes over tens to hundreds of thousands of years. They show that levels of greenhouse gases in the atmosphere are closely linked to global temperatures. Rises in temperature are accompanied by an increase in the amount of greenhouse gases.

These ice cores also show that, over the last 350 years, greenhouse gases have now rapidly increased to levels not seen for at least 800,000 years and very probably longer. Modern humans, who evolved about 200,000 years ago, have never previously experienced such high levels of greenhouse gases.

Natural Fluctuations in Climate
Over the last million years or so the Earth's climate has had a natural cycle of cold glacial and warm interglacial periods. This cycle is mainly driven by gradual changes in the Earth's orbit over many thousands of years, but is amplified by changes in greenhouse gases and other influences. Climate change is always happening naturally, but greenhouse gases produced by human activity are altering this cycle.

Volcanic eruptions and changes in solar activity also affect our climate, but they alone can't explain the changes in temperature seen over the last century.

Scientists have used sophisticated computer models to calculate how much human activity—as opposed to natural factors—is responsible for climate change. These models show a clear human "fingerprint" on recent global warming.

Climate Models and Future Global Warming

We can understand a lot about the possible future effects of a warming climate by looking at changes that have already happened. But we can get much more insight by using mathematical models of the climate.

Climate models can range from a very simple set of mathematical equations (which could be solved using pen and paper) to the very complex, sophisticated models run on supercomputers (such as those at the Met Office).

While these models cannot provide very specific forecasts of what the weather will be like on a Tuesday in 100 years time, they can forecast the big changes in global climate which we could see.

All these climate models tell us that by the end of this century, without an extremely significant reduction in the amount of greenhouse gases we produce, the world is likely to become more than 3°C warmer than in the 19th century. Note that this is a global average and that regional changes in some places will be even higher than this. There could even be global average rises of up to 6°C which would have catastrophic impacts. This means that our action—or inaction—on greenhouse gas emissions today will have a substantial effect on climate change in the future.

The Effects of Climate Change

We can already see the impacts of climate change and these will become more severe as global temperatures rise. How great the impacts will become depends upon our success in reducing greenhouse gas emissions.

The Effects of Rising Temperatures on the UK

If global emissions are not reduced, average summer temperatures in the south east of England are projected to rise by:

- over 2°C by the 2040s (hotter than the 2003 heat wave which was connected to 2,000 extra deaths in the UK)

- up to nearly 4°C by the 2080s

Rises in global temperature will have both direct and indirect effects on the UK. The UK's food supplies could be affected as crops in the UK and overseas could fail or be damaged by changes in temperature, rainfall and extreme weather events.

These extreme weather events in the UK are likely to increase with rising temperatures, causing:

- heavier rainfall events—with increased risk of flooding

- higher sea levels—with larger storm waves putting a strain on the UK's coastal defences

- more and longer-lasting heat waves

The Effect of Warming on Rainfall Patterns and Water Supplies

Changing rainfall patterns will affect water supplies. Too much rainfall in some areas and not enough in others will contribute to both flood and drought conditions. We are already seeing increasing numbers of heavy rainfall events, and expect this increase to continue, with greater risk of river and flash flooding.

Mountain glaciers are expected to continue melting which, along with reduced snow cover, will put stress on communities that rely on these as sources of water.

Changes in the Oceans

Increasing temperatures and acidification of the oceans are threatening sea life around the world. Coral reefs in particular will be at major risk if ocean temperatures keep increasing.

Sea levels will keep rising as the polar ice sheets and glaciers melt and the warming oceans expand. Even small increases of tens of centimetres could put thousands of lives and properties at risk from coastal flooding during stormy weather.

Coastal cities with dense populations are particularly vulnerable, especially those that can't afford flood protection.

The Impact of Warming on Food Production

Even with low levels of warming (less than 2°C above the temperature in 1800), global production of major crops such as wheat, rice and maize may be harmed. Though warming may help some crops to grow better at high latitudes, food production in low latitudes will very likely suffer. This will cause a growing gap between food demand and supply.

Because trade networks are increasingly global, the effects of extreme weather events in one part of the world will affect food supply in another. For example, floods or droughts that damage crops in Eastern Europe or the US can directly affect the cost and availability of food in the UK.

The Impact on Ecosystems

Rapid, large changes in global temperatures (4°C or more above the temperature in 1800 by the end of this century) could cause the extinction of entire species. Even with smaller amounts of warming species will be placed more at risk. The animals and plants most at risk will be those that:

- have no new habitats to move to

- can't move quickly to new habitats

- are already under threat from other factors

Extinctions could have an enormous impact on the food chain. Most ecosystems would struggle to live with large changes in climate which happen rapidly within a century or so.

The Impact on Human Health

Climate change is expected to make some existing health problems worse as temperatures increase. Malnutrition could become more widespread as crops are affected and warmer temperatures could increase the range of disease-carrying insects. Vulnerable people will be at risk of increased heat exposure, although there will likely be fewer health problems related to cold temperatures.

Poverty

Populations with low income in both developed and developing countries will be most vulnerable to the impacts of climate change. Decreasing food production, an increase in health issues associated with climate change, and more extreme weather will slow economic growth, making it increasingly difficult to reduce poverty.

The Impact of Extreme Weather Events Globally

Growing populations and increasingly expensive infrastructure are making our societies more vulnerable to extreme weather events. Heat waves and droughts are expected to become more common and more intense over the coming century, and more frequent heavy rainfall events and rising sea levels will increase the risk of floods.

While not all extreme weather events can be directly linked to human influences, we are already seeing the huge impacts on society that extreme weather events can have. The World Meteorological Organization (WMO) reported that between 2001 and 2010 extreme weather events caused:

- more than 370,000 deaths worldwide (including a large increase in heat wave deaths from 6,000 to 136,000)—20% higher than the previous decade

- an estimated US$660 billion of economic damage—54% higher than in the previous decade

Possible Abrupt Changes in Our Climate

Most discussions of climate change look at what is most likely to happen, such as the likely temperature changes if we do, or don't, take action to reduce greenhouse gas emissions.

But scientists have identified the possibility that with sustained high temperatures major elements of the Earth's climate could be drastically altered. These "tipping points" in our climate are less likely, but potentially much more dangerous.

While known impacts from small temperature rises could be managed (although this will become increasingly expensive as temperatures increase), passing a tipping point could cause large or abrupt changes, some of which may be effectively irreversible.

For example:

- Arctic permafrost could thaw rapidly, releasing greenhouse gases that are currently "locked away" and causing further rapid warming

- the great sheet of ice covering Greenland, which contains enough ice to cause up to 7 metres of sea level rise, could almost entirely melt. While this would take a long time to happen, it is possible that the ice sheet would not be able to regrow after a certain amount of melting occurs.

While such events are considered unlikely, they can't be ruled out, even under relatively low temperature rises of less than 2°C above the temperature in 1800. All indications are that, should we pass one of these tipping points, there would be a range of extremely severe impacts.

Agreement Among Experts

Overwhelming amounts of scientific evidence show that the planet is warming and that human activity is the main contributor to this warming.

Many leading national scientific organisations have published statements confirming the need to take action to prevent potentially dangerous climate change. These include:

- the G8+5 National Science Academies' Joint National Statement which represents the UK, along with Brazil, Canada, China, France, Germany, India, Italy, Japan, Russia and the United States

- the American Association for the Advancement of Science (AAAS) statement

- the Royal Society and US National Academy of Sciences have produced an authoritative and accessible report on Climate Change Evidence and Causes which provides answers to many common questions

You can find out more about the scientific evidence on climate change from:

- The Met Office Hadley Centre

- Frequently Asked Questions from the Intergovernmental Panel on Climate Change

- The UK Geological Society

The Role of the IPCC

The Intergovernmental Panel on Climate Change (IPCC) is an independent body composed of scientists from around the world. It has been tasked by the United Nations to assess and review the most recent scientific, technical and socio-economic evidence related to climate change.

The IPCC's fifth assessment science report concluded that the scientific evidence for a warming climate is undeniable and that "human influence on the climate system is clear."

The UK Government has always fully supported the work of the IPCC and regards its assessments as the most authoritative view on the science of climate change available.

Tackling Climate Change

If we take action to radically reduce greenhouse gas emissions now, there's a good chance that we can limit average global temperature rises to 2°C. This doesn't mean that there will be no more changes in the climate—warming is already happening—but we could limit, adapt to and manage these changes.

If we take action now:

- we will avoid burdening future generations with greater impacts and costs of climate change
- economies will be able to cope better by mitigating environmental risks and improving energy efficiency
- there will be wider benefits to health, energy security and biodiversity

The Economic Benefit of Taking Action Now

It makes good economic sense to take action now to drastically cut greenhouse gas emissions. If we delay acting on emissions, it will only mean more radical intervention in the future at greater cost.

Taking action now can also help to achieve long-term, sustainable economic growth from a low-carbon economy.

UK Government Action

The UK government is:

1. working to secure global emissions reductions

2. reducing UK emissions

3. adapting to climate change in the UK

Climate Change Has Increased the Intensity and Frequency of Severe Weather Events

Union of Concerned Scientists

In the following viewpoint, the Union of Concerned Scientists argues that climate change isn't just limited to extremes of hot and cold; it also causes more severe weather events. This means natural disasters like hurricanes and floods not only become more frequent, they begin to happen in areas that were previously unaffected by them. While it is up to governments to pass laws curbing emissions, citizens must take care of the parts of the globe they call home. The Union of Concerned Scientists believes that weatherproofing our infrastructure and homes is a cost-effective measure for dealing with natural disasters. Good emergency planning in advance of natural disasters does save lives. The Union of Concerned Scientists is a nonprofit organization whose members develop and implement solutions to the planet's most pressing concerns.

As you read, consider the following questions:

1. What kind of severe weather can be expected as rates of global warming rise?
2. How does global warming affect rainfall?
3. What steps can people take in anticipation of severe weather events?

"Is Global Warming Linked to Severe Weather?" Union of Concerned Scientists, June 17, 2011. Reprinted by permission.

Overhead, tall, dense clouds are poised to burst, their presence a sign of an imminent deluge.

These cumulonimbus masses are a reminder of the destructive floods that are occurring around the globe, which, taken together, are potent signals of one of the greatest environmental challenges of our time: global warming.

Powerful rain and snow storms—and, ironically, intense drought periods—are a well-known consequence of a warmer planet.

What Is the Relationship Between Global Warming, Climate, and Weather?

Weather is what's happening outside the door right now; today a thunderstorm is approaching. Climate, on the other hand, is the pattern of weather measured over a number of decades.

Over the past 30 years there has been a pattern of increasingly higher average temperatures for the whole world. In fact, the first decade of this century (2001–2010) was the hottest decade recorded since reliable records began in the late 1800s.

These rising temperatures—caused primarily by an increase of heat-trapping emissions in the atmosphere created when we burn coal, oil, and gas to generate electricity, drive our cars, and fuel our businesses—are what we refer to as global warming.

One consequence of global warming is an increase in both ocean evaporation into the atmosphere, and the amount of water vapor the atmosphere can hold. High levels of water vapor in the atmosphere in turn create conditions more favorable for heavier precipitation in the form of intense rain and snow storms.

The United States Is Already Experiencing More Intense Rain and Snow Storms

As the Earth warms, the amount of rain or snow falling in the heaviest one percent of storms has risen nearly 20 percent on average in the United States—almost three times the rate of increase in total precipitation between 1958 and 2007.

In other words, the heaviest storms have very recently become even heavier. The Northeast has seen a 74 percent increase in the amount of rain or snow falling in the heaviest storms.

As Storms Increase in Intensity, Flooding Becomes a Larger Concern

Flash floods, which pose the most immediate risks for people, bridges and roads, and buildings on floodplains, result in part from this shift toward more extreme precipitation in a warming world.

Regions previously thought to be safe from floods are increasingly threatened by them; agencies such as the National Oceanic and Atmospheric Administration (NOAA), National Aeronautics and Space Administration (NASA), and the US Geological Survey (USGS), among others, are working to gather information that can be used to redraw flood maps to help anticipate vulnerable areas.

In 2008 two scientists, Sharon Ashley and Walker Ashley, of Northern Illinois University, analyzed flood fatalities between 1959 and 2005 in the mainland United States, excluding those from Hurricane Katrina.

Their research found that Texas had the largest number of fatalities from flash floods and river floods over the study period. When standardized for population, South Dakota, Mississippi, West Virginia, and Montana had the highest numbers of fatalities from flooding per 100,000 people. Those between the ages of 10 and 29 and those over 60 years old were disproportionately at risk.

Does Global Warming Create More Frequent and More Intense Tornadoes?

Tornadoes are relatively small, short-lived phenomena and scientists don't have robust enough data to determine whether and how climate change may be affecting tornado frequency, intensity, or the geographic range where tornadoes are most likely to form.

Tornadoes often form when warm, moist air near the Earth's surface rises and interacts with cooler and drier air higher in the atmosphere. This creates unstable conditions that are favorable for thunderstorms and sometimes tornadoes.

Unlike thunderstorms, tornadoes need a rotational source such as when warm, moist air from the Gulf of Mexico wafts over the southeast and strong Jetstream air aloft arrives from a westerly direction, as during the tragic string of tornadoes in April 2011.

While one study found that the number of tornadoes reported in the United States has increased by around 14 per year over the past 50 years, the trend may have more to do with how tornadoes are tracked and reported rather than how many are actually forming.

Similarly, the study found that severity ratings for tornadoes are usually based on the damage they cause to structures and may not have been consistently applied over the past fifty years.

What Can Be Done to Deal with Severe Weather?

This pattern of intense rain and snow storms and periods of drought is becoming the new normal in our everyday weather as levels of heat-trapping gases in the atmosphere continue to rise.

If the emissions that cause global warming continue unabated, scientists expect the amount of rainfall during the heaviest precipitation events across country to increase more than 40 percent by the end of the century. Even if we dramatically curbed emissions, these downpours are still likely to increase, but by only a little more than 20 percent.

Regardless of what actions we take to cut emissions, we must adapt to the likelihood that severe storms are becoming ever more commonplace.

Efforts such as modifying local infrastructure to withstand floods, adjusting agricultural patterns to account for droughts, as well as establishing emergency planning in our homes, would be far less costly to implement when compared to the costs of responding to washed out bridges, deluged homes, or loss of life.

Clearly, the time has come to develop smart planning and engineering solutions to cope with storms of the future.

Rising Temperatures Encourage the Spread of Disease

Michaeleen Doucleff

In the following viewpoint, Michaeleen Doucleff argues that climate change affects health on a global level. One example is the mosquito. When you think of the world's deadliest animals, the tiny mosquito probably isn't the first creature you imagine. But in fact, mosquitoes are the deadliest animal because of their ability to spread devastating diseases like malaria and Zika. Mosquitoes breed in warm climates; as the Earth warms, the population of mosquitoes rises too. Scientists are struggling to understand the link between global warming and mosquito-borne illnesses around the world. As climate change becomes more of a threat to human life, governments have begun to be more responsive. Global efforts to reduce gas emissions and rely more on clean energy are giving scientists hope for the future. Doucleff is a reporter for National Public Radio's Science Desk.

As you read, consider the following questions:

1. How is climate change affecting the mosquito population?
2. Why do mosquitoes pose a threat to humans?
3. What do scientist think is contributing to the rising rates of mosquito-borne illness?

F or decades, scientists have been making predictions about how climate change will hurt health around the world.

But actually showing a link? That's been pretty tough.

Take for example, mosquito-borne diseases. It's easy to blame rising temperatures for the global spread of Zika or the explosion of dengue fever. Mosquitoes thrive in higher temperatures, right?

Yes and no. As we reported earlier this year, warmer weather doesn't necessarily mean mosquitoes are more likely to spread viruses like dengue, yellow fever and Zika. Higher temperatures can actually reduce transmission of viruses because the insect's lifespan can decrease in warmer weather. So the mosquito may die before the virus has time to mature and become infectious inside of it.

In other words, climate's connection to health is extraordinarily complicated.

Now [an] international team of scientists has taken a step toward untangling this problem on a global scale.

"All of the work we present is pretty tricky," says Dr. Nick Watts, at University College London, who led the study. "I don't think any of us would ever say that this has been easy."

Around the world, people have experienced an average increase in temperature about 1.5 degrees Fahrenheit, and the study— published Monday in the *Lancet* journal—finds several signs that even this small amount of warming threatens the health of hundreds of millions of people each year.

First, the number of vulnerable people exposed to heat waves has surged worldwide, the study finds. In the past few years, about 125 million people over age 65 experienced heat waves each year, compared to about 19 million people each year in the 1990s.

"That's a pretty stunning number," says Kim Knowlton, an environmental researcher at Columbia University, who studies climate change and health but wasn't involved in this study. "Heat waves aren't just an inconvenience. Heat kills." And it also exacerbates existing problems, such heart disease and kidney problems.

What Is Geoengineering?

Climate geoengineering refers to large-scale schemes for intervention in the earth's oceans, soils and atmosphere with the aim of reducing the effects of climate change, usually temporarily. It includes a wide array of techniques centered around blocking sunlight or reflecting it back into space, removing carbon dioxide from the atmosphere, or allowing heat to escape into space.

Geoengineering schemes do not attempt to address the root causes of climate change driven by greenhouse gas emissions. Many geoengineering proposals also do not address other major issues such as pollution, ecological destruction from extreme fossil fuel extraction or ocean acidification. Instead, each one is an attempt to address principally one effect of climate change—global increase in temperature—through additional large-scale changes to the atmosphere, oceans, lands, or even outer space.

Because climate geoengineering proposals represent the intentional efforts to change the climate on a global scale, it's crucial to gather as much information as possible about the risks and potential effects of these techniques.

"What Is Geoengineering?" geoengineeringmonitor.

This recent surge in heat waves is consistent with previous studies looking at health and climate change, including meta-analyses published by the Intergovernmental Panel on Climate Change in 2014. "Rising temperatures have [likely] increased the risk of heat-related death and illness," the IPCC wrote.

The second major consequence of warming temperatures is an increase in weather-related disasters. The frequency of floods, droughts and wildfires, collectively, has increased by 46 percent since the 1980s, rising from about 200 events each year to 300 events per year. And some of that increase is due to climate change, the *Lancet* study finds.

Families around the world—including those in the US— are already experiencing these events firsthand, Knowlton says.

"Communities are hurting. People are reeling globally," she says. "And I think this experience might mark a turning point in the public's perception of climate change because people are connecting the dots to their health, here and now."

Surprisingly, the study finds that deaths from weather-related disasters has not increased during the same time period.

"There's no discernible upward or downward trend in the lethality of these extreme weather events," Watts says. "That may simply be because the data is not over a long enough period of time to isolate that trend."

And then there's the question of mosquito-borne diseases. Since 1990, annual cases of dengue worldwide have doubled each decade. Much of this rise is likely due to rapid urbanization and global travel, the World Health Organization says.

But Watt and his collaborators do find that climate change has contributed to dengue's explosion—at least a little bit.

"We're not trying to say that all cases of dengue fever are the result of climate change," Watts says. "But we've identified a very strong signal in the climate trends that are increasing the capacity of the *Aedes* mosquitoes to spread dengue." Although they don't yet know why.

Specifically, the team estimates that climate change has increased dengue transmission by *Aedes aegypti* and *Aedes albopictus* by 3 percent and 6 percent, respectively, since 1990.

Finally, the *Lancet* study also analyzes what countries are doing to slow down climate change. "That's probably the part of this report that really surprised me," Watts says. "There are glimmers of hope in that data."

For the past 25 years, he says, countries have been basically doing very little to reduce carbon emissions. "Progress has been woefully inadequate."

But now there are signs the tide may be turning by a small degree.

"In the past five years, we have started to see an acceleration in the response to climate change," Watts says.

In particular, the use of coal around the world has slowed down, the study finds and possibly even peaked in 2013. Some countries are relying more on natural gas and some are starting to swap in renewable energy sources—like geothermal, hydropower, ocean energy, solar energy and wind energy—which not only reduce carbon emissions but also make the air healthier for people to breathe.

"That's really exciting," Watt says. "Because we could all use a little bit of hope at the moment."

Coordinated Efforts to Mitigate Climate Change Are Lacking

Ken Caldeira and David W. Keith

In the following exerpted viewpoint, Ken Caldeira and David W. Keith argue that the United States needs federal research programs to address solutions to climate change. The UK and German governments have initiated such coordinated programs. Scientists are currently developing two methods of battling climate change known as carbon dioxide removal and solar radiation management. This cutting-edge technology is aimed at lessening the effects of human-made climate change. The field of geoengineering is still in its infancy, and many of its hypothesis remain untested. However, it does offer humans the best chance at reversing climate change. Caldeira is a senior scientist in the Department of Global Ecology at the Carnegie Institution in Stanford, California. Keith is director of the Energy and Environmental Systems Group at the Institute for Sustainable Energy, Environment and Economy and Canada Research Chair in Energy and the Environment at the University of Calgary.

As you read, consider the following questions:

1. What are the two types of geoengineering strategies?
2. What are the goals carbon dioxide removal and solar radiation management?
3. Which geoengineering strategy should governments be focusing on?

"The Need for Climate Engineering Research," by Ken Caldeira, David W. Keith, University of Texas at Dallas, Fall 2010. Reprinted with permission from ISSUES IN SCIENCE AND TECHNOLOGY.

Like it or not, a climate emergency is a possibility, and geoengineering could be the only affordable and fast-acting option to avoid a global catastrophe. Climate change triggered by the accumulation of greenhouse gases emitted into the atmosphere has the potential of causing serious and lasting damage to human and natural systems. At today's atmospheric concentrations, the risk of catastrophic damage is slight—though not zero. The risk will probably rise in coming years if atmospheric concentrations continue to increase. Although not everyone agrees with this assessment, it is supported by the bulk of the scientific evidence.

For the moment, the United States and other nations are trying to address this risk by controlling emissions of carbon dioxide (CO_2) and other greenhouse gases into the atmosphere, with mixed success at best. The time may well come, however, when nations judge the risk of climate change to be sufficiently large and immediate that they must "do something" to prevent further warming. But since "doing something" will probably involve intervening in Earth's climate system on a grand scale, the potential for doing harm is great.

[...]

Scientists have identified a range of engineering options, collectively called geoengineering, to address the control of greenhouse gases and reduce the risks of climate change. One class of geoengineering strategies is carbon dioxide removal (CDR), which removes greenhouse gases from the atmosphere after they have already been released. This approach may involve the use of biological agents (such as land plants or aquatic algae) or industrial chemical processes to remove CO_2 from the atmosphere. Some CDR operations may span large geographic areas, whereas other operations may take place at centralized facilities operating in a relatively small area. Another class of strategies is solar radiation management (SRM), which involves a variety of methods for deflecting sunlight away from Earth or otherwise reducing the levels of solar energy in the atmosphere.

These two strategies are radically different. CDR seeks to address the underlying cause of the climate problem: elevated greenhouse gas concentrations. These approaches are not inexpensive and take time to implement at scale. The more promising of these approaches introduce no unprecedented new environmental or political risks and introduce no fundamentally new issues in governance or regulation. Some CDR approaches, such as the planting of forests, are already considered in international climate negotiations.

SRM seeks to diminish the adverse climate effects of elevated greenhouse gas concentrations without addressing the root cause of the problem. The best of these approaches are shockingly inexpensive (at least with respect to direct financial costs of deployment) and can be deployed rapidly. However, they do introduce unprecedented environmental and political risks, and they pose formidable challenges for governance and regulation. No SRM proposal has yet been seriously considered in an international climate negotiation.

Both approaches may contribute to cost-effective environmental risk reduction, yet there are no federal research programs systematically addressing these options. How should such programs be structured? Given that the two strategies are so different, it would make sense for the government to develop at least two research program areas. One should focus on CDR and other options to reduce the concentrations of greenhouse gases that have already been released to the atmosphere. Another program area should focus on SRM and other options to diminish the climate consequences of increased greenhouse gas concentrations. Each of these strategies is examined below.

CDR

Because of the longevity of atmospheric CO_2, managing the long-term risk of climate change will require us to reduce the atmospheric concentration from current levels. Managing emissions is necessary but not sufficient. But CDR can make a difference only if CO_2 is captured on a huge (gigaton) scale. The sheer scale of the challenge means that CDR always will be relatively slow and expensive.

Research on CDR should be divided into four different research programs. Little coordination is needed among these different research activities; they are so different that there is little to be gained by combining the research under a single umbrella. The research programs would focus on:

Biomass with Carbon Capture and Storage

Plants remove CO_2 from the atmosphere when they grow. When burned in power plants to produce energy, plants release their accumulated CO_2, producing power that is roughly carbon-neutral. If the plants are burned in power plants that capture CO_2 and store it underground in geologic reservoirs, then the net effect is to move carbon from the active biosphere to the deep geosphere, reversing the effect of producing and burning fossil fuels This approach is already being investigated within DOE [Department of Energy] and the US Department of Agriculture (USDA), and the interagency cooperation seems to be working well.

Chemical Capturing of CO_2 from Air

Laboratory tests have demonstrated that chemical engineering approaches can be used to remove CO_2 from ambient air. This CO_2 can then be compressed and stored underground in geologic reservoirs. Because the concentration of CO_2 in air is much lower than the concentration in power-plant exhaust gases, capturing CO_2 from air normally would be more expensive than capturing it from power plants. But there are ways around this problem. For example, facilities to remove CO_2 from ambient air could be made more cost-efficient by locating them near cheap but isolated sources of energy, such as natural gas fields located in remote areas. Furthermore, we may be willing to pay high prices to remove CO_2 from the atmosphere should the consequences of high atmospheric CO_2 concentrations prove worse than anticipated. For example, industrial CDR might be seen as preferable to SRM. [Full disclosure: One of us (Keith) runs a start-up company developing this technology.] DOE is the logical choice to lead this research.

Increasing Carbon Storage in Biological Systems

A number of approaches have been suggested for increasing carbon storage in biological systems. These approaches include encouraging the growth of forests and promoting the use of agricultural practices, such as "no-till" agriculture, that foster the storage of carbon in soils. DOE, USDA, and NSF [National Science Foundation] have supported research on some of these methods, and this approach has received some attention in international climate negotiations. However, biological systems are relatively inefficient in their ability to capture CO_2. It is estimated that it would take approximately 2.5 acres of crop land to remove the CO_2 emission from just one US resident—an impractical requirement. But even though these approaches are unlikely to play a leading role in climate mitigation, some techniques may prove cost-effective, especially when the land can be used for multiple purposes or when other benefits may accrue.

It also has been suggested that the biomass accumulated in plant matter could be buried, either on land or at sea, in a way that would ensure long-term storage. Advocates of such methods argue that they would confer a considerable advantage over, for example, growing a forest and leaving it in place. With biomass burial, the same land could be used repeatedly to capture CO_2, whereas a forest grows only once and does not significantly increase its carbon store after it has reached maturity. Farm waste might be another source of material that might be suitable for burial. Overall, however, current evidence suggests that it would make more environmental sense not to bury biomass but to use it in place of coal in electric power plants, which are notorious CO_2 emitters.

In another biological approach, carbon storage in the ocean could perhaps be increased somewhat by fertilizing the ocean with nutrients, such as iron, nitrogen, and phosphorus, which would encourage tiny organisms to bind the carbon in their physical structures. However, most observers have concluded that ocean fertilization is unlikely to be an attractive option that can be deployed at large scale. Fertilizing the ocean with iron to promote storage has received the most attention, because in areas

Geoengineering Isn't a Magic Bullet

There's no planet B. But is there a plan B? Can we save ourselves from the worst effects of climate change? Ideas exist, but there's no magic bullet—hacking the climate may cause more harm than good. We spoke to Riley Duren, a systems engineer based at NASA's Jet Propulsion Laboratory (JPL), to get his take on the topic. Riley looks at how we can use observations of planet Earth to make better-informed responses to climate change.

Geoengineering is an attempt to avoid or reduce the negative consequences of climate change by directly altering parts of the Earth's natural system. It's different from "mitigation" efforts, where people try to reduce emissions of [heat-trapping] greenhouse gases, or preserve natural carbon-dioxide storage or removal mechanisms like forests. It's also distinct from "adaptation," which involves dealing with the impacts of climate change.

Geoengineering is not a cure. At best, it's a Band-Aid or tourniquet; at worst, it could be a self-inflicted wound.

By itself, hacking the climate system won't fix the way society manages the planet, and in fact it can de-incentivize [effective management]. If geoengineering is perceived as a "silver bullet" that offers the illusion of consequence-free carbon pollution, then there's no incentive to control emissions that are the root cause of the problem. Even if geoengineering could be made to work safely, we would have to continuously ramp it up to keep pace with accelerating emissions—and that's not sustainable.

The climate has a lot of inertia; once it starts moving in a certain direction it may be difficult to stop. The carbon we are pumping into the atmosphere today is essentially permanent; natural processes take thousands of years to remove it. There may also be irreversible "tipping points"—cliffs, or points of no return—that could cause dramatic, abrupt climate changes like shifts in ocean circulation or irreversible melting of the Greenland ice sheet.

Generally, we don't understand the risks of geoengineering well. Engineering the planet could make things worse, and it could cause serious social and political issues. All of these things suggest to me that geoengineering should be seen as a highly uncertain insurance policy or emergency response, not a solution.

"Just 5 Questions: Hacking the Planet," by Erik Conway, National Aeronautics and Space Administration, April 14, 2014.

where iron is a limiting nutrient for biological growth, this would probably be the most cost-effective option. However, there are many questions regarding the effectiveness of these approaches in storing carbon for long periods. Furthermore, because the oceans are a global commons, ocean fertilization options, unlike nearly every other CO_2 removal method, raise a range of thorny problems related to governance and regulation. NSF and DOE have funded some studies of ocean fertilization, but the research is now largely dormant. Also, some of the governance issues are being addressed under the London Convention and Protocol, an international effort to protect the marine environment from human activities, and the Convention on Biological Diversity, an international agreement to protect the planet's wealth of living organisms.

Distributed Chemical Approaches
In general, these approaches involve using massive amounts of basic minerals that react with acidic CO_2 to form new stable minerals. These approaches amount to an acceleration of the natural weathering cycle that in the very long run removes CO_2 from the biosphere. One such approach is based on the fact that the CO_2 in seawater is eventually incorporated into solid carbonate minerals within bottom sediments. The rate of these chemical processes can be accelerated by sprinkling finely crushed limestone over certain parts of the ocean. Alternatively, calcium or magnesium oxides can be added to seawater, increasing the water's capacity to hold CO_2 in storage and prevent it from ever returning to the atmosphere. These approaches would also neutralize carbon acidity in the ocean, helping to alleviate a problem known as ocean acidification.

None of these distributed chemical approaches is a magic bullet. There also are a number of environmental concerns, including the scale of mining that would be required. Nevertheless, such approaches might prove cost-effective relative to conventional carbon capture and storage from power plants.

As envisioned, the research programs on CDR might best be housed within DOE, where they would fit neatly into the agency's current carbon capture and storage research program. Preliminary research should focus on assessing the barriers and potential of each proposed approach, including costs and benefits.

[...]

Solar Radiation Management

Earth can be cooled by a variety of engineering methods, some of them more practical than others, given current technology. There are four main classes of SRM proposals, which are described below in approximately decreasing likelihood of feasibility at large scale:

Stratospheric or Mesospheric Aerosols

Small particles high in the atmosphere can potentially scatter or reflect sunlight back to space, exerting a net cooling effect on Earth's climate. However, because of particle aggregation and gravitational settling, it is not clear that such an aerosol layer could be sustained indefinitely. Thus, maintaining this much solar reflection high in the atmosphere could involve spreading material over a broad altitude range or deploying "designer" particles that are less susceptible to aggregation. Further, it would be desirable to be able to control the latitudinal distribution of these particles; ideally, it would be possible to turn them "on" or "off" at will to exert a high degree of geographic and temporal control. The potential for designing such particles is unknown at this time.

Whitening Marine Clouds

It has been proposed that low clouds in some oceanic regions could be whitened with a fine spray of seawater, and if done on a large enough scale, this could cool Earth considerably. This proposal rests on widely accepted understanding of cloud physics and how that physics is likely to affect climate. Two lines of study—on natural gases that emanate from the oceans and on ship exhausts—indicate that the proposed method should work at some level. Initial calculations suggest that the method could conceivably offset 10 to 100% of the global mean temperature increase from a doubling of atmospheric CO_2 concentration.

Satellites in Space

It has been proposed that vast satellites could be constructed in space to deflect sunlight away from Earth. The scale of such an undertaking is so enormous that most observers do not feel that such an effort is likely in this century. Nonetheless, placing a sunblock between Earth and the Sun is a simple and effective conceptual approach to addressing threats from global warming. Such a strategy could potentially be of interest at some point in the distant future if the global community finds the need to construct systems that would deflect sunlight for many centuries.

Whitening the Surface

It has been proposed that whitening roofs, crops, or the ocean surface would reflect more sunlight to space, thereby exerting a cooling influence on planetary temperatures. With regard to crops, there is simply not enough crop area or potential for change in reflectivity for this sector to be a game changer. Similarly, there is not enough roof area for changing roof color to make a substantive difference in global climate change, although whitening roofs in some cases may confer co-benefits (such as reducing cooling costs and helping reduce the urban heat island effect). Various proposals have been made to whiten the ocean surface, stemming back to at least the early 1960s, but the ability to do so has not been demonstrated.

In their current form, the best SRM methods have several common properties: They have relatively low direct costs of deployment, they may be deployed rapidly and are fast-acting, and they are imperfect. They are intrinsically imperfect because greenhouse gases and sunlight act differently in Earth's climate system. Nevertheless, every climate model simulation that has applied some "reasonable" reduction in absorption of sunlight has found that these approaches could potentially diminish most climate change in most places most of the time, at least for a doubling of atmospheric CO_2 content.

[…]

Although SRM efforts might be able to diminish most climate change in most places most of the time, it is also likely that these approaches will harm some people in some places some of the time. People who suffer harm may seek compensation. If militarily or politically powerful, they could seek to prevent continued deployment and thus could generate military or political conflict. Even if environmental benefits exceed environmental damages overall, indirect costs associated with the possible need to compensate those adversely affected could dominate the overall cost picture. It does not even need to be the case that the climate intervention system actually causes the climate damage; if people in a region believe that they are harmed by such a system, this could be enough to motivate conflict.

[...]

Of course, a world that is cooled by the diminished absorption of sunlight is not the same as one cooled by a reduction in greenhouse gas concentrations. For the same amount of cooling, an SRM-cooled world would have less rainfall and less evaporation. SRM could affect Earth's great weather systems, including monsoonal rains and winds. Thus, SRM techniques are not a perfect alternative to greenhouse gas emissions reduction and can at best only partially mask the environmental effects of elevated CO_2. Still, SRM may be the only fast-acting approach to slowing or reversing global warming. Therefore, it may have the potential to become a powerful tool to reduce the risks associated with unexpectedly dangerous climate consequences.

Periodical and Internet Sources Bibliography

The following articles have been selected to supplement the diverse views presented in this chapter.

Kate Connolly, "Geoengineering Is Not a Quick Fix for Climate Change, Experts Warn Trump," *Guardian*, October 14, 2017. https://www.theguardian.com/environment/2017/oct/14/geoengineering-is-not-a-quick-fix-for-climate-change-experts-warn-trump.

Claudia Geib, "Our Climate Is Changing Rapidly. It's Time to Talk About Geoengineering," Futurism, January 12, 2018. https://futurism.com/climate-change-geoengineering/.

Chelsea Harvey, "Cleaning Up Air Pollution May Strengthen Global Warming," *Scientific American*, January 22, 2018. https://www.scientificamerican.com/article/cleaning-up-air-pollution-may-strengthen-global-warming/.

David W. Keith and Gernot Wagner, "Fear of Solar Geoengineering Is Healthy—but Don't Distort Our Research," *Guardian*, March 29, 2017. https://www.theguardian.com/environment/2017/mar/29/criticism-harvard-solar-geoengineering-research-distorted.

Leonardo Martinez-Diaz, "Global Environmental Risks Are Keeping Davos Leaders Awake at Night," World Resources Institute, January 19, 2018. http://www.wri.org/blog/2018/01/global-environmental-risks-are-keeping-davos-leaders-awake-night.

Robinson Meyer, "A Major New U.S. Report Affirms: Climate Change Is Getting Worse," *Atlantic*, November 3, 2017. https://www.theatlantic.com/science/archive/2017/11/a-major-new-us-report-affirms-climate-change-is-getting-worse/544952/.

Eduardo Porter, "Fighting Climate Change? We're Not Even Landing a Punch," *New York Times*, January 23, 2018. https://www.nytimes.com/2018/01/23/business/economy/fighting-climate-change.html.

Matt Simon, "The US Flirts with Geoengineering to Stymie Climate Change," *Wired*, December 11, 2017. https://www.wired.com/story/the-us-flirts-with-geoengineering/.

GLOBALVIEWPOINTS

CHAPTER 2

Current Geoengineering Theories

Solar Radiation Management Involves Both Risks and Benefits

M. Granger Morgan and Katharine Ricke

In the following excerpted viewpoint, M. Granger Morgan and Katharine Ricke argue that while solar radiation management (SRM) is hypothesized to be an effective way to lower the temperature of the Earth, there are many variables to consider. Scientists still don't know what effects SRM would have on the climate aside from a reduction in temperature. One concern is that SRM will lower the temperature too much, potentially causing an ice age. Another concern is that SRM alone will not reverse climate change because it doesn't remove CO_2 from the atmosphere. It is clear that mitigating the effects of climate change will require much study and diverse tactics. Morgan is chair of the International Risk Governance Council and Scientific and Technical Council and head of the Department of Engineering and Public Policy at Carnegie Mellon University. Ricke is a doctoral candidate in Carnegie Mellon's Department of Engineering and Public Policy.

As you read, consider the following questions:

1. What factors stop countries from implementing climate change mitigation tactics?
2. What dangers does SRM pose?
3. Should scientists pursue SRM technology?

"Cooling the Earth Through Solar Radiation Management: The Need for Research and an Approach to Its Governance," by M. Granger Morgan, Katharine Ricke, International Risk Governance Council, 2010. Reprinted by permission.

The problem is not that we don't know how to dramatically reduce the world's emissions of CO_2. We can do that with a portfolio of dramatic improvements in the efficiency with which we use energy to produce goods and services, and the wide adoption of energy sources that do not emit CO_2. Nor is the problem that the world's largest emitters can't afford to make the needed changes. Rather, the problem is threefold:

1. Both in the industrialized and in the industrializing world, there are many pressing short-term issues that demand attention and resources (e.g., economic development, public health and national security). Since the most serious consequences of climate change lie decades in the future, it is expedient to procrastinate;

2. There are powerful short-term economic interests that are investing hundreds of millions of dollars to keep the public confused and thus block the emergence of the needed collective social commitment;[8] and

3. Nobody wants to go first, as any country acting alone faces significant national costs for relatively lower internationally distributed benefits. A few leading developed countries need to start making serious deep cuts. If they did that, then we believe, either as a result of moral suasion or diplomatic and economic pressure, others would be induced to follow. But while there has been a lot of rhetoric, at least until now, national leaders in the major countries have judged that short-term domestic interests and concerns prevent them from taking such a lead.

So, while atmospheric concentrations of CO_2 continue to rise at an ever faster rate, the world has continued to procrastinate. Reducing atmospheric concentrations of CO_2, either by reducing emissions or by scrubbing it directly out of the atmosphere, is an inherently slow process. Making a dent in the problem will take decades. That means that even if the entire world got serious about reducing emissions of CO_2 tomorrow—something that all signs suggest is not about to happen—the world would still likely undergo significant climate change. This will happen both because all of these emissions reductions policies take time to implement and because inertia in the ocean-atmosphere system has already committed the earth to some climate change, the consequences of which are still uncertain.

Solar Radiation Management (SRM)

There is a way to cool the planet quickly. A few times every century, nature provides a practical demonstration of this fact when an explosive volcanic eruption lofts millions of tons of SO_2 gas and ash high into the stratosphere. Once there, the SO_2 is converted into fine sulphate particles. These particles reflect sunlight before it has a chance to penetrate deeper into the atmosphere and get absorbed. For example, the eruption of Mount Pinatubo in the Philippines in 1991 produced global scale cooling of about 0.5°C.

The fraction of sunlight that is reflected back into space is called the "planetary albedo." There is nothing new about the idea of modifying the climate by increasing albedo. Scientists have known for many years that this could be done.[9] However, until very recently, there has been almost no serious research on how to do SRM, on what it might cost, on how well it might work, or what its undesirable side effects and risks might be. We believe that there are two reasons the climate research community has not devoted serious research attention to these issues:

- Scientists have been reluctant to divert scarce research funds away from the urgent task of studying the climate system, climate change, and its impacts.

- Scientists have been legitimately concerned that studying this topic might increase the likelihood that someone might actually do it. Humans have a dismaying track record of changing their intentions as their capabilities change.

Current Geoengineering Techniques Are Cost-Effective but Risky

Geoengineering interventions are large-scale attempts to purposefully alter the climate system in order to offset the effects of global warming. Most geoengineering proposals can be divided into two types: solar radiation management (SRM) and carbon dioxide removal (CDR).

Solar radiation management involves increasing the Earth's reflectivity to reduce the energy absorbed by the earth from the sun. The two most popular proposals for this are to spray seawater into the air to increase the reflectivity of clouds (marine cloud whitening) and to increase the concentration of highly reflective sulphate aerosols in the upper atmosphere (stratospheric aerosol injection). While both these interventions promise to be extremely cost-effective in reducing or averting global warming, it is very difficult to predict other impacts such action will have on the Earth's climate, and these may cause damage to human life comparable to that of the climate change that would have happened otherwise. Furthermore, such interventions require maintained action, and should this be interrupted the results could be catastrophic. Thus, while such interventions might be highly cost-effective in averting the impacts of climate change, the difficulty in fully understanding their effects mean such an approach is risky, and we thus do not recommend donations to organizations focusing on solar radiation management.

Carbon dioxide removal involves the development and deployment of technologies capable of extracting and storing carbon dioxide from the atmosphere. While such interventions are far lower risk than SRM, current estimates give the cost of removing one ton of carbon dioxide at about $500, and this still far exceeds the cost of abating a single ton of carbon dioxide through the methods described in the mitigation strategies section. It is uncertain how far down this cost can be brought with further research. In any case, we currently do not think carbon dioxide removal will be more cost-effective than carbon dioxide emission mitigation.

"Geoengineering," by The American Physical Society, Giving What We Can.

In our view, today the world has passed a tipping point and there are two reasons why it is too dangerous not to study and understand SRM:

1. There is a growing chance that some part of the world will find itself pushed past a critical point where, for example, patterns of rainfall have shifted so much that agriculture in the region can no longer feed the people. Believing this shift is the result of rising global temperatures, such a region might be tempted to unilaterally start doing SRM to solve its problem. If this situation arises, and no research has been done on SRM, the rest of the world could not respond in an informed way.

2. With luck, the major effects of climate change will continue to occur slowly, over periods of decades. However, if the world is unlucky and a serious change occurs very rapidly, the countries of the world might need to consider collectively doing SRM. If this situation arises, and no research has been done, SRM would involve a hopeful assumption that the uncertain benefits would outweigh the uncertain and perhaps unknown costs.

While there is great uncertainty about SRM, we are confident that it has "three essential characteristics: it is cheap, fast and imperfect."[10]

Cheap

The classification of SRM activities as "cheap" doesn't just refer to the low economic costs associated with cooling the planet with these mechanisms, but also to the fact that only a little bit of material is necessary to implement these planetary-scale changes, which can offset the influence of tons of CO_2. For example, under the current understanding of SRM technologies, the mass of fine particles needed to counteract the radiative effects of a doubling of atmospheric CO_2 concentrations is approximately 2.6 million tons per day of aerosol if injected into marine stratus clouds or 13,000 tons per day of sulphate aerosol if injected into the stratosphere. By comparison, to achieve the same radiative effect (whether by artificial or natural means), we would need to remove 225 million tons per day of CO_2 from the atmosphere for 25 years straight.[11]

While few realistic engineering analyses have been done on the economic costs of SRM, a 1992 report of the US National Research Council[12] estimated the potential costs of a programme of stratospheric albedo modification based on the use of a standard naval gun system dispensing commercial aluminium oxide dust to counteract the warming effect of a CO_2 doubling. Undiscounted annual costs for a 40-year project were estimated to be USD100 billion. More recent analyses[13,14] have suggested that well designed systems might reduce this cost to less than USD10 billion per year—clearly well within the budget of most countries, and much less costly than any programme to dramatically reduce the emissions of CO_2.

Fast

While cutting emissions of CO_2 and other greenhouse gases would slow or halt their rising concentrations in the atmosphere, much of the CO_2 released through past emissions will reside in the atmosphere for 100 years or more. In addition, inertia in the climate system means that global temperatures will continue to rise. Reducing planetary temperatures through emissions reductions will take many decades to centuries. In contrast, increasing planetary albedo by doing SRM can reduce planetary temperature in days or months. This fast response cuts two ways. On the one hand, it means that SRM could be used to rapidly cool the planet in the event of a "climate emergency," such as the rapid deterioration of the Greenland ice sheet[15] or the sudden release of large amounts of methane from arctic tundra or the deep edges of the coastal oceans. On the other hand, if SRM were started and then stopped before greenhouse gas concentrations in the atmosphere were drastically reduced, then global temperatures could shoot up dramatically.[16] This would be devastating for many ecosystems.

Imperfect

Because the mechanisms by which blocking sunlight cools the planet are different from those by which greenhouse gases warm it, SRM cannot reverse climate change in a perfect way at either the global or local level. Global warming from rising greenhouse gases changes the level of global precipitation in a number of ways. First, rising global temperatures cause more evaporation. More water vapour in the atmosphere produces more precipitation. But, higher concentrations of greenhouse gases in the atmosphere also modify how the temperature of the atmosphere changes with altitude, dampening the "convective instability" that drives the way that water is cycled in and out of the atmosphere (what scientists call the hydrological cycle). With rising concentrations of greenhouse gases and rising global temperatures, the precipitation-increasing effect dominates and precipitation will increase globally. But, when SRM is used to lower global temperatures in a world with high CO_2, only the dampening effect remains. Thus, SRM necessarily weakens the global hydrological cycle.[17] This effect would affect different regions of the planet differently, with SRM compensating for climate changes in some regions reasonably well and potentially exacerbating changes that would occur with global warming in others. It is almost certain that the benefits and costs of global climate stabilization would not be equitably distributed among regions.[18]

In addition to such imperfections, a number of negative side effects could result from the various proposals for implementing SRM. Injecting aerosols into the stratosphere could provide reaction sites that might lead to significant destruction of stratospheric ozone.[19] And, because SRM does nothing to stop the rise of CO_2 from anthropogenic activity, it will not slow the associated acidification of the surface ocean, the continuation of which could lead to profound changes in ocean and terrestrial ecosystems, including the likely demise of many or all coral reefs.[20]

[...]

The Need for Research and an Approach to Its Governance

In our experience, the reaction of most people when they first hear about SRM is that "messing with the planet" like this is a terrible idea. Indeed, it is tempting to say we should create a global taboo against all efforts to study or engage in SRM, much as we've done for chemical and biological weapons. However, given the very wide uncertainty bounds on our present knowledge about climate change and its impacts, there is unfortunately some small chance that the world will face a global climate catastrophe that places billions of people at risk. If that were to happen, the countries of the world might collectively need to do some SRM to limit the damages. It is also plausible that a major country, suddenly experiencing a serious local or regional climate disaster such as prolonged drought, could decide to do SRM unilaterally, thus imposing its consequences on the entire planet. In both these cases, if the world has not studied SRM and its impacts, it won't be able to make informed decisions or muster informed counter arguments.

[…]

Notes

(8) See for example Naomi Oreskes and Erik M. Conway, Merchants of doubt: how a handful of scientists obscured the truth on issues from tobacco smoke to global warming, Bloomsbury Press, 2010.

(9) In addition to adding small reflective particles to the stratosphere, other methods such as increasing marine cloud brightness or placing mirrors in space, have been proposed. Here we concentrate on reflective particles in the stratosphere, though many of the climatic effects would be similar with other SRM methods.

(10) The quote is from David W. Keith, Edward Parson and M. Granger Morgan, "Research on Global Sun Block Needed Now," *Nature, 463*(28), 426-427, January 2010.

(11) David Keith. "The Case for Geoengineering Research," Presentation at MIT, October, 30, 2009.

(12) NAS Panel on Policy Implications of Greenhouse Warming, *Policy Implications of Greenhouse Warming: Mitigation, adaptation and the science base*, National Academy Press, 918pp., 1992.

(13) A. Robock, A. Marquardt, B. Kravitz, and G. Stenchikov, "Benefits, Risks, and Costs of Stratospheric Geoengineering," *Geophys. Res. Lett.*, 36, L19703, doi:10.1029/2009GL039209, 2009.

(14) S. Salter G. Sortino J. Latham, "Sea-going Hardware for the Cloud Albedo Method of Reversing Global Warming," *Phil. Trans. R. Soc.* A, 366, 3989–4006. doi:10.1098/rsta.2008.0136, 2008.

(15) There is some chance that the loss of much of Greenland's ice might be irreversible once it has started.

(16) Matthews, H. D. & Caldeira, K. "Transient Climate-carbon Simulations of Planetary Geoengineering," *PNAS, 104*, 9949-9954, 2007.

(17) G. Bala, G., P.B. Duffy and K.E. Taylor, "Impact of Geoengineering Schemes on the Global Hydrological Cycle," *PNAS, 105*, 7664-7669, 2008.

(18) See for example: A. Robock, L. Oman and G.L. Stenchikov, "Regional Climate Responses to Geoengineering With Tropical and Arctic SO2 Injections," *J. Geophys. Res., 113*, 2008; or K. Ricke, M.G. Morgan, M. Allen, "Regional Climate Response to Solar Radiation Management," *Nature Geoscience, 3*, 537-541, 2010.

(19) S. Tilmes, R.R. Garcia, D.E. Kinnison, A. Gettelman, P.J. Rasch, "Impact of Geoengineered Aerosols on the Troposphere and Stratosphere," *J. Geophys. Res., 114*, D12305, 2009.

(20) S.C. Doney, V.J. Fabry, R.A. Feely, J.A. Kleypas, "Ocean Acidification: The other CO_2 Problem," *Annu. Rev. Marine. Sci., 1*, 169-192, 2009.

Rushing to Implement SRM Would Be Unethical

Genevieve Wanucha

In the following viewpoint, Genevieve Wanucha argues that, while solar radiation management might be the best option on the surface, the technique could go very wrong. Most scientific experimentation is done in a lab. Geoengineers run computer simulations to test their theories because real-world testing could have catastrophic effects. The scientific community agrees that geoengineering is still years away from real-world testing. But as the number of severe weather events increases, the general population is eager for real steps toward climate change mitigation. Scientists believe that there are still too many unanswered questions surrounding the effects of SRM for it to be tested in the real world. While climate change is a pressing issue, scientists have rightly agreed that rushing a solution would be unethical. Wanucha is a science writer whose work has appeared in Oceans at MIT and NPR.

As you read, consider the following questions:

1. What are the dangers of implementing SRM technology without also lowering CO_2 emissions?
2. What ethical considerations does geoengineering pose?
3. If climate change is an issue now, why are scientists slow to test current geoengineering techniques?

"Future of Solar Geoengineering Far from Settled," by Genevieve Wanucha, MIT News, August 16, 2013. Reprinted by permission.

A t "Debating the Future of Solar Geoengineering," a debate hosted last week by the MIT Joint Program on the Science and Policy of Global Change, four leading thinkers in geoengineering laid out their perspectives on doctoring our atmosphere to prevent climate change.

The debate featured Stephen Gardiner of the University of Washington, David Keith and Daniel Schrag of Harvard University, and Alan Robock of Rutgers University. Oliver Morton from the *Economist* ran the show as a deft and witty moderator.

The debate focused on the easiest, fastest and cheapest geoengineering option on the table: solar radiation management. This technique would involve intentionally injecting sulfate aerosols into Earth's upper atmosphere, the stratosphere. These aerosols, which are the same particles released by volcanic eruptions, would reflect sunlight away from Earth, cool the planet, and, in theory, stabilize climate.

While climate modeling shows that solar radiation management would reduce risks for some people, there are a number of reasons why this technique might be a bad idea, Robock said. For instance, pumping particles into the stratosphere could shift rainfall patterns and chew up the ozone layer, thus tinkering with the amount of water and UV light reaching human and ecological systems. "We are going to put the entire fate of the only planet we know that can sustain life on this one technical intervention that may go wrong?" he challenged.

Robock's stance is what Keith called "the very common, intuitive, and healthy reaction that geoengineering is 'nuts' and we should just get on with cutting emissions." But Keith and Schrag systematically picked the argument apart as they made the case that, even in the most optimistic of scenarios, we may not be able to solve the climate problem by acting on greenhouse gas emissions alone. For them, geoengineering is a real option.

Humans are burning enough fossil fuels to put 36 billion tons of CO_2 into the air every year. And because the gas stays in the atmosphere for incredibly long time periods, we're already

Will CO$_2$ Reduction Be Enough to Save Coral Reefs?

How much carbon dioxide is too much? According to United Nations Framework Convention on Climate Change (UNFCCC) greenhouse gases in the atmosphere need to be stabilized at levels low enough to "prevent dangerous anthropogenic interference with the climate system." But scientists have come to realize that an even more acute danger than climate change is lurking in the world's oceans—one that is likely to be triggered by CO$_2$ levels that are modest by climate standards.

Ocean acidification could devastate coral reefs and other marine ecosystems even if atmospheric carbon dioxide stabilizes at 450 ppm, a level well below that of many climate change forecasts, report chemical oceanographers Long Cao and Ken Caldeira.

Atmospheric CO$_2$ absorbed by the oceans' surface water produces carbonic acid, making certain carbonate minerals dissolve more readily in seawater. This is especially true for aragonite, the mineral used by corals and many other marine organisms to grow their skeletons. For corals to be able to build reefs, which requires rapid growth and strong skeletons, the surrounding water needs to be highly supersaturated with aragonite.

"Before the industrial revolution, over 98% of warm water coral reefs were surrounded by open ocean waters at least 3.5 times supersaturated with aragonite," says Cao. "But even if atmospheric CO$_2$ stabilizes at the current level of 380 ppm, fewer than half of existing coral reefs will remain in such an environment. If the levels stabilize at 450 ppm, fewer than 10% of reefs would be in waters with the kind of chemistry that has sustained coral reefs in the past."

For the ecologically productive cold waters near the poles, the prospects are equally grim, says Cao. "At atmospheric CO$_2$ levels as low as 450 ppm, large parts of the Southern Ocean, the Arctic Ocean, and the North Pacific would experience a rise in acidity..." Under those conditions the shells of many marine organisms would dissolve, including those at the base of the food chain.

"If current trends in CO$_2$ emissions continue unabated," says Caldeira, "in the next few decades, we will produce chemical conditions in the oceans that have not been seen for tens of millions of years. We are doing something very profound to our oceans. Ecosystems like coral reefs that have been around for many millions of years just won't be able to cope with the change."

"Modest CO$_2$ Cutbacks May Be Too Little, Too Late for Coral Reefs," Science X,
September 22, 2008.

committed to global warming far into the future. "Climate is going to get a lot worse before it gets better," Schrag said. "We have to push for emissions reductions, but the world is going to put a lot more CO_2 in the atmosphere, and we better figure out what to do about it."

But solar radiation management, Keith and Gardiner agred, would not be ethical in the absence of a simultaneous reduction in CO_2 emissions. As computer simulations by University of Washington researchers indicate, if we were to inject aerosols for a time, while continuing to emit CO_2 as usual, a sudden cessation of the technique for any reason would be disastrous. The aerosols would quickly fall to natural levels, and the planet would warm at a pace far too rapid for humans, ecosystems and crops to adapt.

"So if, as a result of decisions to implement solar engineering to reduce risks now, we do less to cut emissions and emit more than we otherwise would, then we are morally responsible for passing risk on to future generations," said Keith.

Caveats to geoengineering continued to roll in during the debate's Q&A session. The technique would likely end up a dangerous catch-22 in the real world, according to Kyle Armour, a postdoc in MIT's Department of Earth, Atmospheric and Planetary Sciences: "The case can be made that the times we would be most likely to use solar radiation management, such as in a climate emergency, are precisely the times when it would be most dangerous to do so." In essence, implementing geoengineering to tackle an unforeseen environmental disaster would entail a rushed response to a misunderstood climate system with uncertain technology.

The post-debate reception was abuzz with conversations about the issue. Several MIT graduate students noted that the debaters never touched upon the most fundamental research needed to evaluate the viability of geoengineering: aerosol effects on clouds.

Aerosols in the stratosphere do reflect sunlight and exert a cooling effect on Earth. "But they have to go somewhere," said MIT's Dan Cziczo, an associate professor of atmospheric chemistry who studies how aerosols, clouds and solar radiation interact in

Earth's atmosphere. "Particles fall down into the troposphere where they can have many other effects on cloud formation, which have not been sorted out. They could cancel out any cooling we achieve, cool more than we anticipate, or even create warming."

Indeed, the most recent Intergovernmental Panel on Climate Change (IPCC) report lists aerosol effects on clouds as the largest uncertainty in the climate system. "I don't understand why you would attempt to undo the highly certain warming effect of greenhouse gases with the thing we are the least certain about," Cziczo said.

The panelists acknowledged that scientists don't understand the technique's potential effects well enough to geoengineer today —but they have no plans to give up hope. Keith noted a need for a memorandum laying out principles of transparency and risk-assessment, as well as vastly expanded research programs for geoengineering. "Before we go full scale," Keith said, as the debate came to a close, "we have to broaden far beyond the small clique of today's geoengineering thinkers, but that doesn't have to take decades."

CO_2 Removal Technology Still Years Away

Bobby Magill

In the following viewpoint, Bobby Magill argues that geoengineering techniques are still far in the future. As you have read, scientists do not believe SRM can work on its own. Promising research shows that SRM and CO_2 removal could help reverse the damages of climate change. For CO_2 removal to work, scientists need to find a way not only to remove carbon from the atmosphere but also store it once it's been removed. Scientists are currently testing a variety of ways to store and use carbon, but all of these projects are still in their infancy. Some scientists worry the rate of climate change might outpace that of scientific innovation. Magill is a journalist and president of the Society of Environmental Journalists. Previously, he was senior science writer covering energy and climate for Climate Central.

As you read, consider the following questions:

1. What are "negative emissions"?
2. Why do scientists believe humans need to cease using fossil fuels?
3. What are some of the problems scientists need to solve before they can put carbon removing technology to use?

Climate pollution equal to about 27 times humans' 2015 carbon dioxide emissions may have to be removed from the

"A Cooler Future May Hinge on Removing CO_2 from the Air," by Bobby Magill, Climate Central, April 20, 2017. Reprinted by permission.

atmosphere and locked underground forever in order to keep the globe from warming beyond 1.5°C (2.7°F) above preindustrial levels, according to a new study.

The research, led by scientists at the International Institute for Applied Systems Analysis, or IIASA, in Austria, adds to the mounting evidence that countries will have to physically remove carbon dioxide from the atmosphere to prevent global warming from exceeding dangerous levels.

Removing carbon dioxide from the atmosphere is called "negative emissions," and it's central to the Paris climate agreement, which aims to prevent the globe from heating beyond 2°C (3.6°F). One of the main goals of the agreement is to keep warming to 1.5°C, a goal growing more difficult as the US and other countries waver on their commitments to cut emissions.

Human greenhouse gas emissions will have to peak globally within 10 years for the 1.5°C target to be met, according to the study.

"Emissions need to peak very soon because the CO_2 emitted now doesn't disappear, or stop trapping heat, even if we were to reach full decarbonization," said the study's lead author Brian Walsh, a former IIASA researcher now consulting for the World Bank. "Emissions need to not only peak but begin a rapid decrease soon in order to have a plausible shot at meeting the 1.5°C target."

Turning emissions around so quickly will involve humans completely weaning themselves from fossil fuels use by around 2050 and widely implementing negative emissions techniques, Walsh said.

Glen Peters, a global carbon cycle researcher at the Center for International Climate Research in Norway, who is unaffiliated with the study, said emissions need to fall as fast as they have increased in recent years, something that will take ever-more heroic efforts if climate pollution is to peak within a decade.

"It's hard to see 2°C without some sort of negative emissions," he said.

The study suggests that as fossil fuels are phased out, people may have to remove and permanently store an exagram of atmospheric carbon dioxide, or roughly 27 times the carbon that humans emitted in 2015. Globally, humans emitted about 36 billion metric tons of carbon dioxide that year, according to European Commission data.

But the researchers say that negative emissions on such a large scale "remains a distant reality."

Most computer models forming the basis of the Paris pact's emissions cuts assume that humans will be actively removing carbon dioxide from the atmosphere on a large scale by late this century. But much of the technology that would reduce atmospheric carbon concentrations is in its infancy, has never been proven to work on a large scale and the hazards associated with it are largely unknown.

Negative emissions techniques under development include directly capturing emissions and storing them underground, planting more trees to store carbon dioxide in their trunks and roots, and, among other methods, engineering forests to store more carbon than they would naturally.

The technique the IIASA study considers most promising is called "biomass energy with carbon capture and storage," or BECCS. That technique involves growing trees and plants on a large scale to be burned in biomass power plants whose carbon emissions would be captured and safely stored underground.

BECCS and other methods requiring planting large new forests are controversial because it's unclear how they would alter ecosystems, displace people and be effective in actually cutting emissions. Some scientists have called the potential risks a significant "moral hazard," while others pointed to research showing that cutting down trees to burn as biomass energy does nothing to remove carbon dioxide from the global carbon cycle.

The study says that if BECCS and other negative emissions technologies prove to be uneconomical or unfeasible, the only alternative is for people to completely stop using fossil fuels as soon as possible.

But Peters said countries' ability to develop negative emissions technology quickly enough to make a dent in climate pollution is doubtful.

"At the moment, it's hard to see a business model and pathway that would make negative emissions technologies feasible at scale," Peters said.

"These are big technologies in that it takes time to plan, approve, and build the capture facilities, not to mention the time and logistics to characterize carbon storage sites," he said. "These time lags would suggest the large scale roll out would not happen for 10 years even if we started planning today. Even if we figure out the technology in the next decade, then it may be too little too late, unless we have deep mitigation already ongoing."

But Walsh said that when societies have accepted the full costs of emitting carbon, including the social cost of carbon and the costs of measures to cut climate pollution and develop negative emissions technology, they'll begin to pour more money into finding ways to reach the Paris targets.

"It could be that we're nearing a tipping point in terms of climate change consequences and public understanding thereof," he said. "And when we get there, I have no trouble believing the policy, funding and technology will follow quickly."

We Should Proceed with Solar Geoengineering—Cautiously

Garth Heutel

In the following viewpoint, Garth Heutel maintains that solar geongineering can be part of an optimal climate policy. Heutel modifies an economic model to reach his conclusion, arguing that an evaluation of costs and benefits has been sorely lacking in the debate of geoengineering's potential risks and benefits. The author believes that solar geoengineering can prevent a tipping point, or a point from which we can no longer recover from the damage done by global warming. Heutel is assistant professor of economics at Georgia State University and a faculty research fellow at the National Bureau of Economic Research.

As you read, consider the following questions:

1. What is an example of a greenhouse gas, as mentioned in the viewpoint?
2. What is an IAM?
3. What is a tipping point, as referenced by the viewpoint author?

There are a number of ideas for how people might intentionally alter the planet's climate system—an approach called geoengineering. One of the most frequently discussed ideas is solar geoengineering, blocking some of sun's energy by, for example, injecting tiny particles called sulfate aerosols into the atmosphere. But solar geoengineeering remains a controversial method of addressing climate change.

And while much has been written about its potential benefits and its potential drawbacks, relatively little work has been done systematically evaluating those costs and benefits.

In a pair of working papers, my coauthors, Juan Moreno-Cruz and Soheil Shayegh, and I modify an economic model that is designed to create the optimal climate policy to include geoengineering.

We find that solar geoengineering can play an important role in the near-term in keeping both costs and temperatures low. But in the long run, optimal policy must involve eliminating greenhouse gas emissions.

Cheap But...

The Earth is getting warmer because of the greenhouse gases like carbon dioxide that humans are emitting into the atmosphere. The most direct way to solve this problem is to stop emitting those gases.

There are two problems with that solution, though. First, it isn't cheap or easy to do so right now, since so much of our economy depends on fossil-fuel-fired, greenhouse-gas-emitting energy. Second, even an immediate halt to all such emissions wouldn't stop the warming that is already "baked in" to the planet, since greenhouse gases remain in the atmosphere, warming the planet, for decades.

There is a solution to global warming that avoids both of those problems: solar geoengineering (SGE). SGE can reduce temperatures by blocking a fraction of incoming sunlight in order to offset the warming caused by greenhouse gases. The sunlight can be blocked by creating sulfate aerosols (sulfur-rich particles) in the stratosphere to act as tiny reflectors. This mimics what happens to the climate naturally after large volcanic eruptions.

SGE is cheap—up to 100 times cheaper than reducing greenhouse gas emissions. It can work fast—reducing temperatures nearly instantaneously.

However, this technique comes with drawbacks. It does not reduce greenhouse gas concentrations in the atmosphere or the oceans, and thus it does nothing to address ocean acidification. It may also have unexpected negative side effects, like affecting tropical monsoons.

Models and Scenarios

To evaluate these costs and benefits, we use a tool called an integrated assessment model (IAM). An IAM includes both an economic model and a climate model to analyze the effect of the climate on the economy, the effect of the economy on the climate, and of policy interventions.

For example, an IAM will tell you what the optimal level of emissions reductions is once you input the costs of reducing emissions and the damages caused by temperature increases. IAMs typically demonstrate a "ramping-up" of climate policy—modest levels of emissions reductions now, with increased intensity in the future.

However, IAMs typically do not model solar geoengineering. We modified a commonly used IAM called DICE to include SGE as an alternative policy option. In the original version of DICE, the only policy available is abatement—reducing carbon dioxide emissions. In our modified DICE model, policymakers can also choose to use SGE. SGE will reduce temperatures, and it will do so more quickly than will abatement, but it will not reduce carbon concentrations.

Although not the first to incorporate SGE, our model is the first to systematically solve for the optimal mix of abatement and SGE. Also, we carefully calibrate the costs, benefits, and risks of SGE based on the most recent state-of-the-art scientific analysis.

This is important because substantial uncertainties remain, in particular over the side-effect damages from SGE, like the effect that a shortened monsoon season could have on food production. For these highly speculative damages, our model is more conservative. It assigns even higher values to the damages from SGE than previous models.

Our model also captures the crucial fact that, because SGE does not reduce carbon concentrations, it cannot remedy any damages that come directly from rising levels of carbon, including ocean acidification. In other words, we modeled SGE as a substitute for abatement, but recognized it as an imperfect substitute.

Buying Time

The results from our base-case analysis confirm what others have written about optimal SGE deployment: it can "buy time" by allowing us to defer costly abatement while keeping temperatures in check. But it cannot fully replace the need to eliminate carbon emissions.

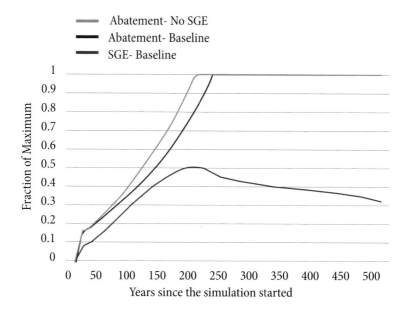

In the image above, we simulate optimal policy far into the future, over the next 500 years. Two different scenarios are represented. In the first scenario, SGE is omitted, and the only policy option is abatement. This is shown in the curve on the left, which gives the optimal abatement intensity over time.

The second scenario is our base case, which includes both abatement and SGE as policy options. The center curve represents optimal abatement in this scenario, and the curve on the right is the optimal intensity of SGE.

The graphs show that when allowed, SGE is used in the near term, and as a result, the amount of abatement that is required is slightly less than in the case where SGE is omitted. When SGE is used, the optimal abatement intensity (expressed as a percentage of carbon emissions that are abated) is up to 25% lower compared to the scenario where SGE is omitted (the difference between the red curve and the blue curve). However, even in the base case where SGE is used, abatement is also used and eventually reaches 100%—all carbon emissions are eliminated. The date at which this occurs is pushed back by about three decades when SGE is used—this is the "buying time" of SGE.

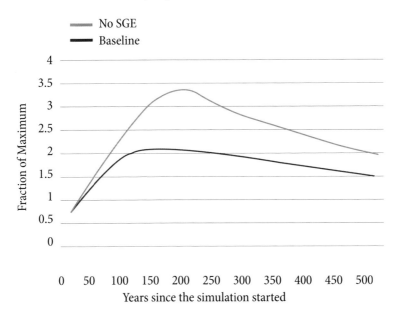

Although more carbon is being emitted into the atmosphere when SGE is allowed, temperature increases are kept substantially lower. This is shown in the graph on the previous page, which compares temperature increases (in degrees Celsius relative to preindustrial temperature) under our base case scenario and under the no-SGE scenario. Without SGE, temperature peaks at about 3.5 degrees Celsius above pre-industrial levels, while SGE keeps this increase to just 2C (3.6 degrees Fahrenheit). (Note that the two-degree optimal temperature increase is derived from the parameters of the model, and it is only a coincidence that it matches the two degrees target that is often discussed by policymakers and the media.)

Tipping Points

SGE can also be an effective way to prevent the climate from reaching a tipping point, an irreversible and very costly change in the climate system caused by global warming. Like much about the climate system, there is a great deal of uncertainty about these tipping points: whether they exist, at what temperature they are reached and how costly they would be once reached.

In an extension to our main analysis, we include the possibility of reaching a tipping point. We model three different types of tipping points and consider three different policy regimes for SGE: ban it, allow it or allow it but only after the tipping point is reached. We find that allowing SGE from the onset is an effective way of managing the risk of reaching a tipping point. Banning SGE or allowing it only once the tipping point is reached only increases society's exposure to tipping point risks, since by definition the tipping points are irreversible.

Next Steps

Our analysis provides concrete, numerical justification for many of the policy ideas that have been merely speculative until now: solar geoengineering can reduce costs, suppress temperature increases, and lessen tipping point risks. But, SGE is not a perfect substitute for abatement, so eventually we must transition to a carbon-free society.

Of course, our results should be interpreted with caution. There are substantial uncertainties about SGE and more research is warranted. IAMs themselves may be misleading, too.

We are not nearly ready to begin solar geoengineering on a large scale, but it seems likely that solar geoengineering will be an important part of our optimal policy toolkit to combat global warming.

Periodical and Internet Sources Bibliography

The following articles have been selected to supplement the diverse views presented in this chapter.

Allison Eck, "Should We Intentionally Manipulate the Earth's Climate?," *NOVA*, January 26, 2018. http://www.pbs.org/wgbh /nova/next/earth/should-we-intentionally-manipulate-the -earths-climate/.

Jeff McMahon, "As Humans Fumble Climate Challenge, Interest Grows in Geoengineering," *Forbes*, September 24, 2017. https:// www.forbes.com/sites/jeffmcmahon/2017/09/24/interest -rises-in-geoengineering-as-humans-fail-to-mitigate-climate -change/#60f91f6f6472.

Robinson Meyer, "What Happens If We Start Solar Geo-Engineering—and Then Suddenly Stop?," *Atlantic*, January 25, 2018. https://www.theatlantic.com/science/archive/2018/01 /what-happens-if-we-start-geo-engineeringand-then-suddenly -stop/551354/.

Eduardo Porter, "To Curb Global Warming, Science Fiction May Become Fact," *New York Times*, April 4, 2017. https://www .nytimes.com/2017/04/04/business/economy/geoengineering -climate-change.html.

Matt Simon, "How Engineering Earth's Climate Could Seriously Imperil Life," *Wired*, January 22, 2018. https://www.wired.com/story/how -engineering-earths-climate-could-seriously-imperil-life/.

Andrew Snyder-Beattie, "Geoengineering Is Fast and Cheap, but Not the Key to Stopping Climate Change," *Guardian*, May 15, 2017. https://www.theguardian.com/sustainable-business/2015 /may/15/geoengineering-climate-change-greenhouse-gases.

Jack Stilgoe, "Can Volcanoes Tackle Climate Change?," *Guardian*, April 10, 2015. https://www.theguardian.com/environment/2015 /apr/10/can-volcanoes-tackle-climate-change-frankenstein -mount-tambora.

Greg Walters, "Geoengineering the Climate Could Cause Devastating African Droughts," *Seeker*, November 16, 2017. https://www .seeker.com/earth/climate/geogengineering-the-climate-could -cause-massive-african-droughts.

GLOBALVIEWPOINTS

CHAPTER 3

Why a Global Effort Is Needed

The Whole World Must Cooperate When Battling Climate Change

Jennifer Morgan

In the following viewpoint, Jennifer Morgan argues that the climate community must use lessons learned from studying other regimes when undertaking current negotiations. These include arms control and trade. The author suggests that thinking outside the box and rethinking definitions of progress can help world leaders tremendously when it comes to addressing climate change. In addition, in what is perhaps the most radical suggestion, Morgan contends that to remove politics from climate change policy has many benefits. Morgan was global director of the World Resources Institute.

As you read, consider the following questions:

1. Why is it helpful to remove political bodies from discussions of climate change?
2. What could potentially spur a "race to the top" of climate change?
3. What are some of the challenges that come with climate change being a multigenerational issue?

Solving climate change is one of humankind's greatest challenges. Caused largely by the burning of fossil fuels, which currently underpin most of modern society's energy system, the solutions are economically, politically and socially complex. In addition, the problem's transnational and transgenerational nature contributes further to the challenge of creating positive coalitions for change and forging agreements among nations to act now for benefits later.

Thus, it is not surprising that the international climate negotiations have moved slowly. Yet, the threat of climate change requires urgent action and creative thinking—in a field where new ideas are often immediately shot down due to one political sensitivity or another.

A Major New Report: Building International Climate Cooperation

In that context, the World Resources Institute is releasing a major new report, *Building International Climate Cooperation: Lessons from the weapons and trade regimes for achieving international climate goals*, which aims to bring fresh thinking into the international climate space at a time when innovative ideas and new approaches are desperately needed.

While it is clear that negotiations within the United Nations Framework Convention on Climate Change (UNFCCC) have catalyzed greater action than would have happened otherwise, it is also clear that those actions are not enough to close the emissions gap and keep global average temperature increase within safe levels. The pledges of the 2009 Copenhagen Accord, and subsequent decisions in Cancun and Durban to embed and monitor those pledges, coupled with the establishment of a new Green Climate Fund, are useful, but so far inadequate.

The Durban Platform, which sets countries on a course to conclude a new climate agreement in 2015, is an important step to address the ever-growing gap between what the science demands and what countries are willing to deliver, but it also offers an opportunity to step back, assess what has worked and what hasn't, and create a new agreement that drives greater change.

The climate community would be wise to study other regimes that could hold relevant lessons for the climate negotiations, and to seek out new ideas that can be pursued within the UNFCCC, or as complementary action outside the UN process. Representing all nations, including the most vulnerable, it is clear that the UNFCCC is likely the place where a multilateral and binding agreement must be made, but this does not require that everything be done there.

In Building International Climate Cooperation, WRI looks outside the climate regime to arms control and trade regimes for inspiration and ideas on how countries can come together to address immense global challenges. To do so, we commissioned papers from top experts who have worked on those regimes—Barry Blechman and Brian Finlay from the Stimson Center and Thomas Cottier from the World Trade Institute—about relevant lessons they found for the climate regime. WRI authors Ruth Greenspan Bell and Micah S. Ziegler then pulled out key findings from both regimes and identified lessons for climate.

For example, in the area of verification there were a number of noteworthy items:

- Verification procedures can become more stringent over time;
- Formal complaint procedures and sanctions play an important role in motivating countries to meet commitments;
- Clear benefits of international cooperation can lead countries to engage with a regime and, in the process, agree to verification procedures or forego some aspects of their sovereignty; and
- Verification can take the form of unilateral and multilateral processes operating in parallel.

Beyond verification, other important lessons include:

- Progress can be made even when major players stall or sit on the sidelines;
- Progress is not solely conditioned by legal form. The study of the weapons and trade regimes suggest it is possible to

achieve substantive outcomes and build both mutual trust and increasingly robust verification processes, even before countries reach a formal, ratified agreement;

- Decoupling issues and outsourcing elements of the regime to specialized bodies can increase progress;

- Variable geometry (differences in commitment levels resulting from allowing Parties who wish to go further and faster the flexibility to move ahead) can spur a race to the top;

- Smaller-scale agreements, for example segmenting out parts of larger challenges or working with a smaller number of countries for specific purposes, can be used to pilot forms of agreement and related verification methodologies, and expand on multilateral verification systems; and

- Setting principles for "graduation" is challenging, but doing so can allow for agreements to evolve and grow as necessary over the long term. Making such arrangements can require regime participants to strike an appropriate balance between equity and environmental integrity in international regimes, taking into account the participants' differing capabilities, needs, and stages of development.

The climate challenge is too big to fail. Yet, if policymakers do not step up with much bolder and more ambitious commitments soon, it will likely be too late. Hopefully, these new ideas can spur some innovation, creativity and greater will to more effectively address this pressing global threat.

Results of Past International Environmental Agreements

Council on Foreign Relations

In the following excerpted viewpoint, the Council on Foreign Relations (CFR) argues that lack of leadership by central players in the climate change debate—especially the United States—has elicited increasing concern about the long-term prospects of the global climate change regime. While climate change may not seem like a foreign policy issue, the need for international cooperation makes it one. The CFR explains how the economic condition of nations can affect their ability to combat climate change. It also explores some of the problems with past international environmental agreements. This kind of research can help governments create stronger environmental agreements in the future. The CFR is an independent organization, think tank, and publisher dedicated to education about the foreign policy choices facing the United States and other countries.

As you read, consider the following questions:

1. How do a country's finances affect its commitment to climate mitigation?
2. Would an international environmental monitoring agency infringe on national sovereignty?
3. Should wealthy nations be obligated to help developing nations combat climate change?

"The Global Climate Change Regime," Council on Foreign Relations, June 19, 2013. Reprinted by permission.

Climate change is one of the most significant threats facing the world today. According to the American Meteorological Society, there is a 90 percent probability that global temperatures will rise by 3.5 to 7.4 degrees Celsius (6.3 to 13.3 degrees Fahrenheit) in less than one hundred years, with even greater increases over land and the poles. These seemingly minor shifts in temperature could trigger widespread disasters in the form of rising sea levels, violent and volatile weather patterns, desertification, famine, water shortages, and other secondary effects including conflict. In November 2011, the International Energy Agency warned that the world may be fast approaching a tipping point concerning climate change, and suggested that the next five years will be crucial for greenhouse gas reduction efforts.

Avoiding the worst consequences of climate change will require large cuts in global greenhouse gas emissions. Humans produce greenhouse gases by burning coal, oil, and natural gas to generate energy for power, heat, industry, and transportation. Deforestation and agricultural activity also yield climate-changing emissions.

One way to reduce emissions would be to switch from fossil-fuel-based power to alternative sources of energy, such as nuclear, solar, and wind. A second, parallel option would be to achieve greater energy efficiency by developing new technologies and modifying daily behavior so each person produces a smaller carbon footprint. Additionally, retrofitting buildings and developing energy-efficient technology greatly help curb greenhouse gas emissions. All such measures, however, engender significant costs, and the onset of the global financial crisis has placed serious new constraints on national budgets both in the developed and developing worlds. Some climate change experts have expressed concern that the ongoing global financial crisis could defer action on climate change indefinitely.

Even if such reforms were implemented, substantial efforts will still be required to adapt to unavoidable change. Recent climate-related events, such as the flooding in Pakistan and Thailand, have caused focus to fall on adaptation financing for developing countries, which could support infrastructure projects to protect vulnerable areas. Other efforts might include drought-tolerant farming.

Distribution of global emissions reinforces the need for broad multilateral cooperation in mitigating climate change. Fifteen to twenty countries are responsible for roughly 75 percent of global emissions, but no one country accounts for more than about 26 percent. Efforts to cut emissions—mitigation—must therefore be global. Without international cooperation and coordination, some states may free ride on others' efforts, or even exploit uneven emissions controls to gain competitive advantage. And because the impacts of climate change will be felt around the world, efforts to adapt to climate change—adaptation—will need to be global too.

At the launch of the United Nations Framework Convention on Climate Change seventeenth Conference of Parties (COP-17) in Durban, South Africa, many climate change experts were concerned that the Kyoto Protocol could expire in 2012 with no secondary legally binding accord on limiting global emissions in place. This fear, however, was somewhat assuaged as the nearly two hundred countries present at the COP-17 approved an extension of the protocol through 2017 and potentially 2020. A decision was also reached at the meeting to draft a successor accord to the Kyoto Protocol by 2015, which would ultimately come into force in 2020. Delegates also envisioned that the new accord would include greenhouse gas emissions targets for all countries, regardless of their level of economic development. This framework notably contrasts with that of the Kyoto Protocol, which primarily focuses on reducing emissions emanating from developed countries.

Despite these and other marked successes during the COP-17, the perceived lack of leadership by central players in the climate change debate—especially the United States—has elicited increasing concern about the long term prospects of the global climate change regime. Additionally, Canada's December 2011 decision to withdraw from the Kyoto Protocol—based on domestic economic concerns as well as its view that the world's top greenhouse gas emitters have refused to ratify the accord—has generated concerns that the Kyoto Protocol itself may be in danger of collapse. Both of these concerns and many other issues will likely be a part of the agenda for the COP-18, scheduled for November 2012 in Qatar.

Overall Assessment: An Underdeveloped and Inadequate System

The current centerpieces for multilateral action against climate change are the United Nations Framework Convention on Climate Change (UNFCCC), its associated Kyoto Protocol, the Copenhagen Accord, and the COP-17 Durban Platform for Enhanced Action ("Durban Platform"). The Kyoto Protocol includes firm commitments to curb emissions only from developed countries, but does not include the United States, and has no meaningful consequences for noncompliance; it has also come under unprecedented strain as Canada officially withdrew from the accord in December 2011. Specifically, Canada's environment minister suggested Canada could only be a part of an accord which includes all major emitters as parties. As Japan and Russia could soon follow Canada's example, the hopes for a legally binding climate accord—even if desirable—may be fading. Additionally, the regime, which allows for numerous exemptions regarding greenhouse gas emissions, fails to provide emerging big emitters like China and India with meaningful targets and incentives to curb their emissions. The architecture for global climate governance looks particularly shaky after the fifteenth Conference of Parties (COP-15), in Copenhagen, failed to overcome entrenched differences among the major parties and deliver targeted emissions cuts. Following Copenhagen, COP-16, in Cancun, made some strides toward effective multilateral action, but the regime still falls well short of promoting needed action to effect positive change, including committing to a post-Kyoto framework.

Similarly, little progress was made during the COP-17 meeting in Durban. While parties agreed to extend the Kyoto Protocol until at least 2017 as well as solidified an operating structure for the

Green Climate Fund, little was clarified concerning the form of a successor accord to the Kyoto Protocol. Delegates to the COP-17 did agree, however, that the new accord would include reduction targets for all nations, rather than exclusively those considered to be developed.

Although delegations at Durban, Cancun, and Copenhagen developed reporting mechanisms, funding pledges, and unilaterally declared country-specific emissions reduction goals, the ongoing lack of an international enforcement body has left these promises largely empty.

The limitations of the Durban Platform, as well as the increasingly tenuous status of the Kyoto Protocol, have created a fresh imperative for global action on climate change. The tension between developing and developed countries is fueled by ongoing disagreements over how to interpret a fundamental underpinning of the UNFCCC and Kyoto framework—namely, the principle of "common but differentiated responsibilities" among industrialized (Annex I) and developing (non-Annex I) countries, particularly when it comes to establishing and achieving meaningful mitigation targets. The 2010 UN climate change summit in Cancun did not achieve a comprehensive international framework, nor did it expect to. The agenda was pushed to the 2011 meetings in Durban, South Africa, where the Kyoto Protocol was extended for another five years at least. Concerns, however, arose over the refusals of India, China, and the United States to unequivocally accept legally binding emissions targets at the meeting, placing doubt on the extent that other significant greenhouse gas emitters will participate in the new commitment window.

At the most basic level, countries disagree over climate monitoring and financing stipulations in the Kyoto Protocol and other legally binding accords. Climate frameworks struggle to effectively monitor greenhouse gas outputs, especially in developing countries. Many countries lack the domestic capacity to audit their total emissions; even if they are able to monitor national levels, some fear that reporting such numbers would encourage international pressure to cap their emissions. Others, like China, argue that an international monitoring system represents an infringement on national sovereignty and that developing states should be afforded some leniency in emissions as they are currently in critical stages of economic development.

Additionally, the climate regime does not adequately address the sources of financing needed to help developing countries cope with climate change. While the meeting in Copenhagen witnessed political progress, including pledges by industrialized countries to provide $100 billion by 2020 to developed countries and the Green Climate Fund was put into place at Cancun, concrete funding streams have yet to materialize. While the COP-17 attempted to clarify how the Green Climate Fund would operate and disperse funds, little firm monetary support was allocated to the mechanism. To date, the total disbursed funds for climate change initiatives, both within and outside of the UNFCCC, add up to only $2.1 billion.

Seeking a more flexible and effective approach, the United States and other emitters have begun to turn to "à la carte multilateralism," focusing on smaller, less formal frameworks, such as the Major Econonomies Forum (MEF) and the Group of Twenty (G20). The MEF was launched in March 2009 as a successor to the Bush administration's Major Economies Meeting (MEM). The seventeen-member MEF, which includes countries responsible for approximately 80 percent of global emissions, has provided an arena for major emitting countries to confront tricky issues and hammer out viable strategies without entering the labyrinth of UN diplomacy. In February 2012, a six-state coalition was also established to tackle climate and public and health risks posed by short-lived pollutants including methane, hydrofluorocarbons, and black carbon (soot). Even these niche fora, however, are not immune to political rancor over legally binding emissions cuts.

Despite concern that alternative efforts to the UNFCCC process might undermine the credibility and success of that universal forum, the MEF and the parallel G20 have the potential to complement the UN track by enabling meaningful dialogue among the countries whose financial commitments and solutions on mitigation and technology truly matter. The MEF and G20 offer leaders a setting for candid dialogue where parties can meet to negotiate new bilateral and "minilateral" arrangements, align parallel domestic initiatives and regulatory approaches, and monitor each other's progress as part of an informal, "pledge and review" process. Accomplishments of the MEF and G20 include, respectively, launching a Global Partnership on Clean Energy Technologies and reaching an agreement to phase out inefficient fossil fuel subsidies. In September 2011 the MEF reportedly held a "frank discussion" regarding the COP-17 meeting in Durban and the future of the Kyoto Protocol among other issues.

Beyond the UNFCCC process and minilateral forums like the MEF and G20, climate change is increasingly addressed by a host of other international actors whose primary mandate may not explicitly include climate change. Within the UN system alone, some twenty agencies work on climate change, often through their own specific lens. The implementation of projects, for example, is spread across institutions like the United Nations Environment Program (UNEP), the Global Environment Facility (GEF), the United Nations Development Program (UNDP), and the World Bank, which work alongside bilateral agencies on mitigation and adaptation projects in developing countries. Although a proliferation of actors focused on this agenda is not necessarily negative, the lack of coordinated policies and programs can be a problem when it leads to redundancy. In part, this fragmentation reflects the inherent complexity of climate change, which has substantive connections to many issue areas, including development, finance, public health, energy, and security.

Understanding Climate Change Threats: Strong but Could Be Improved

The international climate regime is at its strongest when it comes to understanding the threats posed by climate change. Such efforts, which are centered on the Intergovernmental Panel on Climate

Change (IPCC), predate any other dedicated element of the regime. Yet, the infiltration of politics into the climate change debate has hampered the legitimacy and pervasiveness of new findings.

The IPCC was created in 1988 to review, assess, and synthesize the world's scientific information related to climate change. It periodically releases assessment reports, which synthesize global data on climate change. The IPCC reports are central in policy discussions of climate change, and their estimates play an outsized role in setting benchmarks for international action. The IPCC also produces occasional reports on urgent subjects such as carbon capture and technology transfer.

The IPCC is not without its critics, however, and a series of scandals concerning the methods of its reporting has somewhat weakened its legitimacy. Some have accused its reports of being politically driven—their summaries must be signed off on by all member governments—and overplaying the state of agreement on man-made climate change. Reacting to the findings of an independent review, the IPCC introduced institutional reforms in May 2011 to address some of these concerns. That said, the findings of the panel generally concur with those of major scientific associations, such as the US National Academy of Sciences. Within the community of experts on climate science, few believe that IPCC reports overestimate the state of the problem.

The IPCC has also been criticized, from the other side, for underplaying the risks of extreme climate change, again because of the need for political consensus. Similarly, it has been criticized as lagging behind the current state of science because of its long and bureaucratic approval process. At a time when many studies are raising the possibility of extreme climate change, this may tend to bias the IPCC conservatively.

International cooperation on scientific observation and analysis has also benefited from several other forums for sharing global climate data. These include the Group on Earth Observations (GEO), a group of eighty governments committed to creating a

Global Earth Observation System of Systems (GEOSS) as a common source for detailed data on everything related to climate change.

Despite these gains in researching, analyzing, and understanding climate change, a great deal of basic scientific work remains in clarifying the state of scientific opinion on the anthropogenic causes of climate change and ways to mitigate their effects. In addition, the international community needs to expand cooperation efforts in collecting data on the effects of climate change to facilitate adaptation and early warning systems.

Curbing Emissions: Some Progress, but Too Few Commitments

Many countries with mandatory targets under the Kyoto Protocol are on track to cut their greenhouse gas emissions, and large emitters such as China, India, and Brazil suggest that they will take voluntary steps to control levels of anthropogenic pollution. But despite these successes, the existing climate regime remains grossly inadequate when it comes to stabilizing greenhouse gas levels; moreover, regulations that have already passed or which are about to go into effect, like the EU airplane tax, continue to stir significant political controversy. Additionally, the December 2011 Durban Platform committed UNFCCC parties to establish a more universal post-Kyoto accord with "legal force," and in December 2012 at the UNFCCC COP-18, parties agreed to extend the Kyoto commitment period to 2020 and to enter into negotiations for a treaty to replace the Kyoto Protocol in 2015. However, not all parties agreed to this second round of commitments and major emitters like Canada and Japan opted out.

The variance between commitment and action remains an obstacle to the development of a comprehensive solution. The non-binding Copenhagen Accord did little to force country-by-country accountability and action. The 2010 Cancun Agreement brought greenhouse gas reduction pledges under the auspices of the UN Framework Convention on Climate Change, but it remains to be seen if Cancun's call for international assessment of implementation of these mitigation efforts will lead to substantive gains beyond the status quo. A shift in focus from diplomatic discussion over pledges to implementation is one positive outcome of the Cancun Conference.

The IPCC has called for a reduction in emissions to limit the increase in global temperatures by 2 degrees Celsius (3.6 degrees Fahrenheit). Although leaders at Copenhagen and Cancun used the same number to determine their mitigation pledges, the current growth in emissions, absent significant action on climate change, will cause an average global temperatures of 5 degrees Celsius (9 degrees Fahrenheit), according to the most recent analysis produced by the Climate Interactive Scoreboard.

The core policy and regulatory instruments to curb greenhouse gas emissions exist at the national level, and performance therefore varies from country to country. At the international level, the Kyoto Protocol provides three mechanisms that can help countries control their emissions through flexible arrangements. The Clean Development Mechanism (CDM) allows industrialized countries to invest in climate-friendly projects in poor countries and earn carbon credits in exchange. The Joint Implementation (JI) mechanism enables industrialized countries to invest in climate-friendly projects in other industrialized countries and earn carbon credits in exchange. Lastly, emissions trading creates a market for trading carbon credits with countries that are over their target.

From the beginning, the most promising of the three was the CDM, which provides twin benefits of curbing emissions and facilitating economic development for non-Annex I countries. However, experts have pointed to inadequacies regarding its operations and its inability to deliver lower emissions at acceptable costs. In particular, the CDM is burdened with extensive bureaucratic entanglements that have delayed the actual registry of many preapproved projects. More seriously, critics blame the CDM for earning some companies heaps of carbon credits for low-cost changes, noting that national regulation or other means of financing emissions reductions might have been better alternatives. Additionally, some experts complain about China capturing a significant number of the carbon credits, known as Certified Emission Reductions (CERs), at the expense of other developing countries. However, China's extensive participation may also help jump-start its renewable sector, which could have ancillary long-term benefits. Although the COP-17 did not resolve all of these concerns, it did extend the CDM to include carbon capture storage projects—a move that enjoys significant private sector support.

Emissions trading, most developed within the EU framework, has also faced a barrage of criticism. Carbon markets are still in their infancy and fraught with challenges related to price discovery, price volatility, and exposure to political risk. At this stage, some businesses argue that the price of carbon is too low to support profitable opportunities. Similarly, environmental activists argue that capital markets are too unregulated and unstable to serve as a foundation for global efforts against climate change. Despite the value of Europe's carbon market approaching an estimated $120 billion in 2010, concerns remain about the future of the global carbon market absent a legally binding emissions accord.

The G20 has stressed the importance of market mechanisms to fight global warming, and some have argued that carbon markets can be seen as a cheap and simple way to ensure emissions reductions. When reinforced by regulation, such as the mandatory cap-and-trade system in Europe, emissions trading can be a beneficial mechanism that contributes to overall emissions reductions. The EU carbon market, for example, has an estimated value of $120 billion. Similar to the EU model, nine states in the mid-Atlantic and northeast United States have created a market-driven mandatory framework, called the Regional Greenhouse Gas Initiative (RGGI), to reduce emissions. To date, this is one of the most promising initiatives for emissions reduction in the United States.

Outside the Kyoto regime, international efforts to reduce carbon dioxide emissions have led to a UN program on Reducing Emissions from Deforestation and Degradation (UN-REDD). The program provides financial incentives for poor countries to protect their national forests and thereby assigns them with some responsibility for global emissions reduction. By some estimates, tropical deforestation accounts for 15 percent of annual global carbon dioxide emissions. The Kyoto Protocol, however, did not have any mechanism for conservation or prevention of deforestation as a means for mitigating climate change. Under the protocol, countries could seek credits and financial support after forests were cut down but no support was available to prevent them from cutting forests down in the first place. Fortunately, activism on the issue has generated enough interest for industrialized countries to commit $3.5 billion to provide funding for deforestation activities. Similarly, the COP-17 established a technical framework for facilitating deforestation products. Furthermore, in February 2012, the United States, along with Canada, Mexico, Sweden, Ghana, and Bangladesh, launched a joint effort to mitigate short-lived climate pollutants—such pollutants stay in the atmosphere only briefly, but they account for approximately of 30 percent of global warming—such as black carbon, hydrofluorocarbons, and methane. A limited fund of $15 million was set up to support the group's efforts, but heavy emitters like China and India did not sign up.

Monitoring and Enforcing Emissions Curbs: Monitoring Patchy but Improving, Enforcement Nonexistent

Transparency in emissions cuts has become a relatively new focus of the climate change regime. The Bali Action Plan adopted new monitoring parameters that required both developed and developing countries to commit to mitigation actions that could be measured, reported, and verified (MRV). Strengthened somewhat at Copenhagen, this agenda was furthered in Cancun, where the final document called for "international assessment of emissions and removals related to quantified economy-wide emission reductions targets" for developed countries in a transparent manner. However, this language on enforcement has yet to be matched by a plan of implementation, likely making it a contentious issue for future international climate agreements. The 2011 Durban Platform may have created additional confusion regarding the enforcement of climate accords. Particularly ambiguous was its call for a new agreement with "legal force" to replace the Kyoto Protocol rather than one that is expressly "legally binding."

Under the current UNFCCC framework, developed countries report their emissions annually and developing countries are supposed to report theirs every six years. Emissions inventories in developed countries are generally agreed to be strong, and are accepted as the basis for international emissions trading (in which errors in emissions accounting would result in large financial transfers). Reporting from developing countries is widely considered to be much weaker, and the six-year reporting requirement is often violated. The exceptions are CDM projects, which are carefully monitored to determine whether promised emissions reductions are actually being achieved; here, monitoring is widely agreed to be strong. In an effort to improve monitoring, in 2009 the UNFCCC produced a new pledge and review process. This process tasks countries to publish emissions reductions goals in line with their national capabilities and then submit to international monitoring under the Copenhagen Accord.

The barriers to improving emissions monitoring in developing countries are threefold. First, many such countries lack the domestic capacity to monitor their own emissions, which makes international monitoring even more difficult. Existing emissions estimates are generally extrapolations based on energy use, and even large developing countries such as China and India, for example, do not know their total emissions output. This uncertainty is exacerbated in countries with significant emissions from deforestation because the technical means to precisely measure such emissions do not yet exist. Second, even if developing countries are able to monitor their emissions, many are wary that reporting emissions would open them to pressure to cap those emissions—something they have strongly resisted. Third, countries such as China publically state that concessions for an internationally verifiable monitoring system are a direct infringement on their national sovereignty. Despite these barriers, an agreement that focuses on emissions monitoring might be easier to implement than an arrangement based on binding emissions reductions.

Enforcement, meanwhile, is essentially nonexistent. Countries that fail to meet their Kyoto targets are legally required to subtract that shortfall (plus a 30 percent penalty) from their total allowed emissions in the next phase of the protocol. In practice, though, this is meaningless, given that future allowed emissions have not yet been negotiated. If the Kyoto Protocol penalty rules are observed— something still in question—countries could simply negotiate new caps that are inflated by an amount that offsets the penalty or just formally withdraw from the accord as Canada did in 2011.

Financing Emissions Cuts: Needs Concrete Options

Channeling funds to curb emissions and adapt to global warming is one of the thorniest challenges in the fight against climate change. The Green Climate Fund, set forth in Cancun to be a centralized hub for climate financing, only recently agreed in October 2011 on a draft plan for dispersing funds. While the COP-17 made progress in clarifying the governance structure of the Green Climate Fund, only $50 million was promised as seed funding. And, despite Annex I countries having shown significant leadership COP-16 to the UN climate convention by committing to facilitate private funding and provide $100 billion annually in multilateral assistance by 2020 and reconfirmed their commitment to do so at COP-18. Despite this recommitment, however, no framework was agreed upon for financing in the final outcome document. Furthermore, some critics argue that the $100 billion assistance funding should be a base figure, as it falls short of what developing countries require, which is projected to increase to $300 billion per year by 2020.

Total commitments for reaching the $30 billion in short-term funds pledged for 2012 have nearly reached the target amount, but reports indicate that little of this represents money outside of previously existing aid packages. In February 2010, UN Secretary-General Ban Ki-moon established the High-Level Advisory Group on Climate Change Financing to explore means of accomplishing Copenhagen funding pledges. The group's final report was released in November 2010 and calls for taxes on emissions, trading, and international travel. While tangible policy responses concerning the report have been mostly lackluster in the United States, the EU has instituted a controversial emissions tax on airlines flying in and out of its EU territory, which entered into force in January 2012.

Recently, the International Energy Agency (IEA) reported that achieving climate goals by 2020 would require an investment of roughly $5 trillion. The situation becomes particularly vexing when the transfer of money from industrialized countries to developing countries comes into play. At the September 2009 G20 meeting in Pittsburgh, leaders proposed significant increases in funding to poor countries, but differences in how to achieve this goal led to a weak statement that merely recognized the need for climate change financing (for which there was no follow-through at the Toronto G20 summit in June 2010). More recent pledges made at the UN climate conference in Cancun are short of the aspirations of some world leaders and lack details regarding their source and disbursement.

Currently, some climate change financing comes by way of official development assistance (ODA). Several multilateral funds have been established under the UNFCCC, the World Bank, and the GEF to provide grants and loans targeting specific aspects of climate change, ranging from adaptation to development of clean technology. However, by and large these funds are voluntary and have limited differences.

Many experts have pointed to private investments as a way forward. Private investment has been critical in industrialized countries but much harder to come by in developing countries. The Clean Development Mechanism (CDM), initially set up by the Kyoto Protocol, has been applauded for injecting private-sector funding for clean energy projects into developing countries and helping industrialized countries meet their emissions-cutting targets. However, the CDM has brought little benefit to areas most in need of clean energy, notably sub-Saharan Africa.

Some economists and policymakers have proposed innovative solutions to the financing deficit such as a Tobin tax on financial transactions or a carbon tax on air transportation (the EU instituted the latter in 2012). The Organization for Economic Cooperation and Development (OECD) has reported that if all industrialized countries used carbon taxes or auctioned emissions-trading permits to reduce their emissions by 20 percent in 2020 relative to 1990 levels, fiscal revenues could reach 2.5 percent of GDP by 2020.

Utilizing Carbon Sinks: Achievements in Deforestation

Approximately one-fifth of global emissions come from land use, including deforestation. Mitigating the effects of climate change will require looking at a broad set of alternatives, including leveraging tools inherent to our natural ecosystem. Forests provide natural carbon sinks that help mitigate the effects of carbon dioxide emissions. There are currently few initiatives that compensate countries that promote this natural process. Through the CDM, the UNFCCC regime provides carbon credits for afforestation and reforestation projects. Although this is a positive step, critically missing are incentives for forest conservation activities that would help reduce emissions from existing carbon stocks.

In an effort to bridge this gap, numerous bilateral and multilateral arrangements outside the UNFCCC framework have been created to provide assistance to developing countries in harnessing their carbon sinks. Negotiations at the fifteenth meeting of states party to the UN climate convention, for instance, secured a pledge for

$3.5 billion to combat deforestation in developing countries, which complements an existing UN-REDD program funded by Norway, Denmark, and Spain. Additionally, the World Bank Forest Carbon Partnership Facility provides better forestry management and conservation. At the national level, some governments have established funds, such as Brazil's Amazon Fund, and Burkina Faso's cash bonus tree-planting program, which leverage private donations and government resources to provide incentives for the preservation of forests.

Additionally, there has been some attention on promoting oceans as a natural carbon sink. However, scientific skepticism on the ocean's ability to absorb carbon dioxide emissions remains.

Promoting Low-Carbon Development: Needs Coherence, Financial Support, and Developing-Country Buy-In

Low-carbon development must be at the heart of any successful climate change mitigation effort. Yet it faces two distinct challenges. The world is not particularly good at development assistance beyond climate change, and it has no large-scale experience with low-carbon development.

The Kyoto Protocol focused on promoting low-carbon development through the Clean Development Mechanism (CDM). Although the CDM has undoubtedly resulted in some low-carbon investment that would not have otherwise occurred, it has not prompted fundamental shifts in development patterns. Alongside it, traditional development organizations have begun to invest in low-carbon development. The World Bank, for example, has ramped up climate-related spending, and the UNEP has set climate change as a priority in its capacity-building efforts. These efforts are constrained, however, by funding that is not commensurate with the scale of the challenge, as well as by deeper challenges in the development aid model. These international institutions are also not well coordinated, with occasionally weak mechanisms that can fail to complement each other.

Another important path to low-carbon development is new technology, such as carbon capture and storage (CCS), which focuses on securing and storing carbon dioxide emissions before they are released into the atmosphere. Although this technology is still in its early stages, successful pilot projects offer hope of developing and implementing it for large-scale projects. Some countries are committed to implementing variations of it, and both bilateral and multilateral cooperation is under way. This cooperation is particularly important because implementing CCS on a large scale can be expensive and offers few obvious economic benefits. One of the major multilateral efforts in this area is the Carbon Sequestration Leadership Forum (CSLF), which supports joint efforts to develop cost-effective carbon sequestration technology. At the bilateral level, the EU-China Partnership on Climate Change helps to develop Near-Zero Emissions Coal (NZEC) plants in China using CCS technology. The United States and China have also recently agreed to develop joint projects using CCS technology. Additionally, an international initiative, Futuregen, led by the US Department of Energy, harnesses public and private-sector funds and expertise to help build near-zero emissions plants around the world.

Renewable and nuclear energy will be critical in diminishing reliance on fossil fuels and developing low-carbon communities. Expectations for nuclear power as an alternative source of energy are especially high among big emitters such as India, China, and the United States, as well as in a number of developing countries that lack the necessary infrastructure to meet their growing energy needs. Since the nuclear incident in the wake of Japan's March 2011 earthquake and tsunami, some of the support for nuclear power has declined. Currently, the International Atomic Energy Agency (IAEA) assists countries in determining whether nuclear energy is a feasible option. When nuclear energy is optimal, the agency assists with energy planning and developing relevant infrastructure, such as drafting nuclear legislation and establishing independent and effective safety regulators. However, given its limited resources, the IAEA will find it increasingly difficult to meet the growing demands for its services as more developing countries seek help in establishing nuclear facilities.

There has also been significant international action on renewable energy. The International Renewable Energy Agency (IRENA), founded in January 2009, is the first international forum for specifically promoting the use of renewable energy. The UNEP has launched several initiatives, including the Global Bioenergy Partnership (GBEP), to support the deployment of biomass and biofuels, and the Solar and Wind Energy Resource Assessment (SWERA), which seeks to make renewable energy data widely available. Despite these promising international efforts, only about 25 percent of the world's energy is produced through renewable and alternative sources (including hydroelectric, biomass, and nuclear). However, investment in these areas continues to increase (rising seventeen percent to a total of $257 billion in 2011) and more and more countries are setting policy targets for using renewable energy.

Another dimension of the solution is often ignored but is likely, in the long term, to be the most prominent: domestic policy reform in developing countries that encourages low-carbon investment. This might include steps like energy market reform or reduction of tariff barriers to low-carbon technology transfer. International institutions have begun to promote domestic policy shifts through measures like technical assistance provided by organizations like the UNEP and UNDP, discussions on tariff reductions for environmentally friendly technologies through the WTO, and processes aimed at phasing out fossil fuel subsidies spurred through the G20. Some existing institutions, though, may incidentally work against positive developments in this area. The Kyoto Protocol's CDM, for example, may discourage countries from making climate-friendly policy changes by rewarding countries only for activities that go beyond existing national policy. Complicating matters, efforts to promote policy shifts and efforts aimed at providing assistance with clean development are rarely coordinated with each other.

Adapting to Climate Change: Addressed Weakly and Incidentally

Adapting to climate change is currently being addressed incidentally through traditional development aid. Organizations like the World Bank and USAID are working to "climate-proof" their investments. Moreover, most traditional development aid (often aimed at areas like health and agriculture) will help countries become more resilient in a changing climate. Yet the perennial shortfalls in development assistance—both financially and in having the desired policy impact—mean that adaptation assistance invariably falls short as well.

There have been targeted efforts to address adaptation in particular. The Kyoto Protocol's Adaptation Fund, supported by a small tax on CDM credit sales, currently yields funds that are supposed to be spent on adaptation. The fund, however, is severely underfinanced and hobbled by its own bureaucratic governance. The GEF also administers several funds that target adaptation efforts. The Least Developed Countries Climate Fund (LDCF) and the Special Climate Change Fund (SCCF) aim to address long-term efforts for the most vulnerable developing countries. Additionally, the World Bank Pilot Program for Climate Resilience (PPCR) works to integrate adaptation measures into development aid. National Adaptation Programs of Action under PPCR are underway in eighteen countries in the Caribbean, the Pacific, Africa, the Middle East, and Asia. While the World Bank facilitates this and other Climate Investment Funds, it has also provided loans for coal power plants and other projects not friendly to the climate change agenda. Most of these efforts are not distinguishable from other development support, however, making it difficult for a separate adaptation fund to make a big difference in any case.

The sixteenth Conference of Parties in Cancun developed a Cancun Adapation Framework (CAF) to raise the prominence of adaptation measures in the UNFCCC's efforts. The CAF also represented the first formal agreement to establish guidelines concerning capacity building in communities vulnerable to the effects of climate change. Adaptation financing, even after the COP-17 in Durban remains an ad hoc enterprise.

Adaptation efforts are also hurt by the failure of the international community to generate precise predictions on the effects of climate change. The IPCC focuses on long-term projections and on regional or global analyses. Organizations like the UNDP help countries use broader projections in national adaptation planning, and national governments sometimes assist others in such efforts. Whether having governments and international institutions handle these projections offers any benefits is, however, still unclear.

Younger People Are the Future

Dana Nuccitelli

In the following viewpoint, Dana Nuccitelli argues that climate change denial is rapidly coming to an end as younger generations are both better educated and experience more of the negative effects of climate change. The author goes on to report that age is not the only factor; ethnicity and gender also can predict the likelihood of a person's acceptance or denial of climate change. In general, the author believes that future generations will look back and question that anyone denied climate change for so long. This viewpoint was written for the Bulletin of the Atomic Scientists, a nonprofit organization hoping to bridge the divide between the worlds of scientific research, political policy, and the public. Nuccitelli is is an environmental scientist with degrees in astrophysics and physics. He has been researching climate science and economics since 2006.

As you read, consider the following questions:

1. What are the dangers of climate change deniers?
2. What are some of the factors that cause younger people to acknowledge the dangers of climate change?
3. What are some ways corporations benefit from climate change denial?

A record number of Americans now view global warming as a serious threat and blame human activities as the cause.

"The climate change generation gap," by Dana Nuccitelli, Bulletin of the Atomic Scientists, April 21, 2016. Reprinted by permission.

But there is apparently a generation gap out there when it comes to accepting the scientific evidence. And an ethnic gap, a gender gap, and a gap in political leaning—along with whether one can be considered one of society's "haves" or "have nots." So, who are these climate deniers? What is their profile?

A June 2014 *Washington Post-ABC News* poll asked a nationally representative sample of American respondents several questions about their support for climate policies. Specifically, those surveyed were asked whether they would be in favor of government greenhouse gas regulations that increased their monthly energy expenses by $20 per month. Overall, 63 percent of respondents expressed support for the proposed policy, including 51 percent of Republicans and 71 percent of Democrats.

Interestingly, there was a significant age gap among the responses. For Democrats under age 40, support for the policy proposal was 78 percent, as compared to 62 percent over age 65. Among Republicans, 61 percent under age 50 supported the proposed regulations, as compared to 44 percent over age 50. According to a Pew Research Center survey, younger Americans are also more likely to correctly answer that the planet is warming and that this warming is primarily due to human activities.

The Climate Acceptance Age Gap

Unfortunately, there's been little research that investigates the causes of this age gap. It is tempting to speculate that perhaps younger minds are more open to new ideas—such as the potential for humans to alter something as large and complex as the Earth's climate, ushering in a new "Anthropocene" geological epoch. Perhaps our educational system is succeeding in teaching these concepts to younger generations.

In fact, the acceptance of the evidence for human-caused global warming may grow as the climate change curriculum improves in American science classes. The challenge is that teachers are human—which means that their political and religious beliefs sometimes get in the way, as do the cultural biases of the local community in which they teach, and their community's attitudes toward the role of government. A recent survey conducted by the National Center for Science Education found that teachers who identified as Republicans, teachers who regarded the Bible as the actual word of God to be taken literally, and teachers who favored libertarian and small-government views, were all less likely to emphasize the scientific consensus on climate change and more likely to air opposing views in the classroom.

Consequently, this survey of US middle and high school science teachers found that while approximately 70 percent of these teachers spent one to two hours on climate change per course, only 54 percent taught students about the scientific consensus on human-caused global warming. Thirty percent incorrectly characterized climate change as being natural in origin, and 15 percent ignored the origins of climate change or the topic of climate change entirely. Although the survey identified systemic obstacles to teaching about climate change in American classrooms, those obstacles will eventually be overcome, and climate literacy will improve as a result—at least among the younger generation.

Exposure to the opinions of one's peer group may also help explain the climate age gap, as older men are the most common faces of climate denial. For example, in 2009 the American Physical Society was petitioned by 206 of its members (approximately 0.45 percent of its membership) to change its climate position and reject the expert consensus on climate change. An analysis of the petition signatories by John Mashey found that approximately 86 percent were born before 1950 (compared to approximately 40 percent of the society's membership as a whole), and 97 percent were born before 1960 (compared to approximately 60 percent of the overall membership). Climate denial conferences are also disproportionately attended by old white men.

But age is not the only predictor of climate change denial.

The Climate Acceptance Ethnicity Gap

African- and Hispanic-Americans were also more likely to correctly answer the Pew Research Center climate questions—and to express concern about climate change—than white Americans. Fifty-nine percent of Hispanic-Americans and 52 percent of African-Americans understand the reality of human-caused global warming, as compared to just 41 percent of white Americans. And 70 percent of minorities express concern about it, as compared to just 50 percent of white Americans. A 2010 report by Anthony Leiserowitz and Karen Akerlof similarly found that minorities were more likely than white Americans to support regulating carbon dioxide as a pollutant, implementing a carbon cap and trade system, and signing international climate treaties.

The ethnicity gap (and the age gap) can likely be explained in part by certain groups' general preferences for maintaining the status quo. Social scientists have identified what they've termed the "white male effect," describing the fact that white males tend to be less concerned about various sources of risk than minorities and women. Scientists have speculated that this effect largely stems from the fact that mitigating these risks could result in restrictions on markets, commerce, and industry that have historically tended to disproportionately benefit white males. In other words, if you are already doing well from the system, you're less inclined to change it—no matter how much the ice melts and the oceans rise. In their 2011 paper "Cool Dudes," Aaron McCright and Riley Dunlap concluded: "The unique views of conservative white males contribute significantly to the high level of climate change denial in the United States." And climate change denialism is largely—but not exclusively—a US phenomenon.

In fact, their research found that conservative white males who express the highest confidence in their opinions about climate science and risks are the most wrong, and in the most severe denial. McCright and Dunlap concluded that "climate change denial is a form of identity-protective cognition, reflecting a system-justifying tendency." This may also contribute to the age gap, since younger

Americans have not yet benefited from the societal status quo to the same degree as older Americans.

Minorities also tend to be disproportionately affected by the negative consequences of climate change, and realize the benefits of addressing it. For example, minorities are more likely to live in close proximity to coal power plants and their associated air pollution. Cutting carbon pollution would result in fewer coal power plants, and hence cleaner air for these populations. Many minorities have also recently emigrated from countries that are more vulnerable to climate change impacts. In other words, some minority groups (particularly Latinos) are more likely to have "transnational ties," and an awareness of how people in other countries think about and are affected by climate change.

Public Acceptance of Human-Caused Climate Change Will Only Grow

In a new paper my colleagues and I published on April 13 in *Environmental Research Letters*, the authors of seven separate studies on the climate consensus joined together to conclusively demonstrate that 90 to 100 percent of climate science experts and their peer-reviewed research agree on human-caused global warming. We found that consensus rises with greater climate expertise, with a majority of our surveys finding 97 percent consensus among the most-published climate scientists and their peer-reviewed research. Currently, only 12 percent of Americans realize that the expert consensus is so high. We call this discrepancy between public perception and reality the "consensus gap," and it will only shrink over time as more people become aware of just how many experts agree on state of the evidence for human-caused climate change.

Similarly, the impacts of climate change on human society will only become more apparent over time. A recent report by the National Academies of Science concluded that climate scientists can already identify the human activity that caused the intensification of some types of extreme weather like heatwaves, droughts, and heavy precipitation events: heatwaves became hotter, droughts drier, and monsoons wetter. As global warming continues to progress, the associated climate changes, like these extreme weather events, will only become more apparent to the general public.

All the indicators are pointing in the direction of increased public awareness and concern about the dangers of human-caused climate change. Concern is highest among American minority groups, who will outnumber whites within a few decades. It's highest among younger Americans, who will outlive older Americans. And concern will only grow as the climate continues to change, as its associated effects become more severe, and as more Americans become educated about climate science and the 97 percent expert consensus on human-caused global warming.

At the same time, a 2015 paper found that the Republican Party stands alone as the only major political party in the world that rejects the need to address climate change. Given the realities of climate change and growing public awareness and concern, including among the party's own young constituents, this is simply an untenable long-term position. Some have written that climate change is the new gay marriage, an issue on which the Republican Party leadership has taken a stand on the wrong side of history— potentially alienating many voters, particularly among younger generations. The youth vote (18-29 year-olds) has increasingly gone against Republicans since the turn of the century, and research has shown that voters tend to stick with whichever political party they first join.

Climate denial caters to a small and dwindling population of old, white, conservative, American men. As with global temperatures, American acceptance of and concern about human-caused climate change is currently at record levels, and is certain to keep rising in the long-term.

Climate Change Requires Both Global and Local Problem Solving

Mike Muller

In the following viewpoint, Mike Muller argues that the global response to climate change can often be affected by what nations have to gain or lose from a warmer climate. While some nations could benefit from warmer temperatures, others, like India and southern African nations, are already suffering from deadly heat waves and other adverse effects. These nations could benefit from climate change mitigation, which could offer temporary relief. However, for reasons Muller explains, many scientists are fearful of implementing temporary solutions even if they could be lifesaving. Muller is a civil engineer and former director general of the South African Department of Water Affairs and Forestry.

As you read, consider the following questions:

1. How do regional interests affect countries' reactions to climate change?
2. Should countries focus on reducing the local impact of climate change or on global projects?
3. What are scientists' concerns about temporary solutions to climate change?

C limate change is a global problem. But local actions are needed to reduce its impact. Specifically, southern African countries must consider what they can do to protect their interests in the face of growing threats to economies and welfare.

So consider the idea of having a giant sunshade over southern Africa. During the recent heatwave, it would have been wonderful. It could have saved lives and there would have been less evaporation from dams, reducing the impact of the current drought. Crops and livestock would have fared better.

Putting up a global sunshade is feasible, not fanciful. It has already been shown to be an option for California. But it is rarely talked about in polite scientific or policy conversation. This is because it would be geoengineering, a human intervention to alter the climate. Many people consider this to be a step too far. But this must change, not least because human action is already causing the climate to change.

Why Geoengineering Is a Difficult Subject

Discussion about geoengineering has been muted because scientists are uncomfortable about accepting second class solutions. They fear that any effort to moderate the impact of additional CO_2 in the atmosphere will reduce the pressure for action on the cause of the problem.

But Africa must look hard at uncomfortable options or face being left behind by other countries with fewer scruples. Specifically, it is important to consider how regional geoengineering initiatives could help to protect southern Africa from some of the more damaging impacts of climate change.

From the outcome of the COP21 meeting in Paris last year, two key points stand out:

1. All countries made a commitment to take action on climate change to avert a global disaster. This was real progress.

2. But the practical commitments they made were nowhere near radical enough to achieve the goal of reducing global warming quickly enough.

The resulting slow progress means that the southern African region could face prolonged hardship. The consensus is that life under climate change will be hotter, and therefore drier, since evaporation and aridity increase with temperature.

Some Countries Stand to Gain, Some to Lose

Southern Africa needs to take action as a region. Not all regions are affected equally by climate change.

Some countries—Canada and Russia specifically—actually stand to gain from a warmer globe. Millions of hectares of land that is currently frozen will become available for agriculture. This will occur just as food problems arise elsewhere.

Other countries—think Saudi Arabia—would like to put off action as long as possible. This will enable them to use their oil revenues to fund the adaptation that they will need. Coal exporting countries like Australia and South Africa have similar interests.

Yet another group of countries would like adaptation to move faster. This is not always because they are concerned about the impact of climate change. Many in Europe believe that there is money to be made from renewable energy. And they would like everyone to adopt it as fast as possible so that they can make more windmills, install more solar panels and sell more power management solutions.

So regional interests have a strong influence on the approach to climate change. And I contend that South Africa, together with its neighbours, is not doing enough to consider specific regional interests and options. That opinion is based on more than a decade's engagement on climate issues at the United Nation's Commission on Sustainable Development, two COPs, the World Economic Forum and South Africa's National Planning Commission as well as my work on southern Africa's water resources.

The thinking—or rather the lack of it—about geoengineering is one example of regional interests.

Creating Shade

Some geoengineering interventions will only work on a global scale. Proposals to suck carbon dioxide out of the atmosphere are one example. But other interventions work more locally.

It has long been known that the presence of some chemicals in the atmosphere can shield the earth from the heating effects of the sun. This has been demonstrated on numerous occasions when, after erupting volcanoes spewed sulphurous gases and ash, the earth cooled noticeably for a couple of years. The most famous case is perhaps the eruption of Mount Tambora in Indonesia in 1815. This led to 1816 being known as the "year without a summer."

The science to use this effect for geoengineering is now well documented. A leading mind on this is professor Paul Crutzen, who won the Nobel Prize for working out how to fix another global atmospheric problem—the ozone hole.

If sulphur dioxide (SO_2) is used, the amount required for a worldwide solar sunshade could be dosed into the atmosphere using existing passenger aircraft. The payload would be the equivalent of two economy class seats on every flight. Crutzen estimated the cost at between $25 and $50 per developed world citizen. It would be more efficient to dose at higher altitudes but the point is that this is already a feasible option.

What needs to be considered is whether this technology could be used to provide local sunshades. These would not help places threatened by rising sea levels which need warming to be stopped at a global level. But it might well help to reduce the impact of higher temperatures on local agriculture and water resources.

Potential risks need to be considered. The amounts of SO_2 needed are tiny compared to what is generated, more harmfully, by industry and natural sources. But it would be desirable to design and use more benign materials. Fortunately, the science of chemistry is increasingly able to design materials with very

Global Cooperation Is Needed to Combat Climate Change

Around the world, countries are working towards ways to reduce climate change. And while individual countries must take into account local contexts, it is unnecessary to always "reinvent the wheel" with each new solution. Through the South-South cooperation (SSC), UNDP connects various stakeholders to form partnerships across the developing world for pursuing these solutions.

On climate change and environmental sustainability, UNDP delivers a portfolio of US$2.3 billion, supporting over 140 countries in pursuing low-emission and climate-resilient development pathways. A central element of this work is South-South cooperation, as the majority of developing countries are critical players who have joined the middle income club, with impressive economic growth, high savings and investment rates and a larger share of trade in goods and services.

Under the Canada-UNDP Climate Change Adaptation Facility, countries like Cambodia, Cape Verde, Haiti, Mali, Niger and Sudan are learning from each other's national experiences to design and implement adaptation approaches to agriculture and water management. As a result, for example, the countries now have improved climate information systems for informed decision-making and integrated planning approaches. The knowledge sharing has enabled them to test and scale up climate risk management measures and strengthen capacity to access and manage climate finance.

In partnership with Denmark, UNDP is working with China, Ghana, and Zambia on renewable energy technology transfer. For example, the China technology transfer to Zambia specifically focuses on off-grid solutions for those communities located far from the power grid. This spotlight on rural electrification allows the part of the Zambian population that is missing out on development opportunities to enhance their livelihoods and quality of life through the provision of clean, sustainably-produced electricity.

In September this year [2015], the world adopted a common vision for sustainable development. It highlights the strong interrelations of climate change and poverty, and calls for urgent actions to combat climate change and its impact on people and ecosystems.

In the next few weeks, under the United Nations Framework Convention on Climate Change (UNFCCC), countries will ink a new universal agreement in Paris to scale-up such commitments before it is too late for the planet and humanity.

Looking forward, South-South cooperation will play a vital role in the successful implementation of a new global climate agreement, by accelerating development momentum across the South, building resilience and mitigating risk.

"Cooperation and Sharing Can Help Combat Climate Change," by Magdy Martínez-Solimán, United Nations Development Programme, November 27, 2015.

specific properties. Doing this to mitigate climate change needs to become a research priority.

To make such interventions practical, the region needs local science, focused on meeting local needs. And Western scientists have been reluctant to help develop this capacity. I have found British scientists working on climate change very helpful on many other subjects, but not on this regional interventions. And South Africa's scientists are too often guided by global thinking rather than local challenges and opportunities.

Finally, there is the question of implementation. Do we have the means to do the job? Since there would almost certainly be international opposition to regional geoengineering, we would need regional capacity for intervention. Could this be a new role for embattled SAA? It would be helpful to have a national airline to enable us to take a regional decision to protect regional interests.

Such a move could buy time while the underlying problem is properly addressed. Critics who argue that this would simply encourage further delay miss the point. The delays are happening and the consequences need to be addressed. Beyond that, the mere threat of regional geoengineering action could accelerate action to address the underlying causes more effectively.

At the least, the southern African region if not the continent as a whole must discuss regional options. And regional geoengineering will have to be on the agenda. Otherwise Africa will once again find itself at the back of the queue, carrying the burden and the costs while those responsible for our problems profit from our passivity.

Possible Negative Effects of Geoengineering Must Be Considered Before It's Implemented

Jane A. Flegal and Andrew Maynard

In the following viewpoint, Jane A. Flegal and Andrew Maynard combine their expertise on the risks and ethical issues surrounding geoengineering. While it is clear that the environment needs to be stabilized, geoengineering also comes with real risks. Attempts to solve problems in one part of the globe could disrupt weather patterns in other areas, bringing about new problems. How can scientists ethically proceed with research on technology that will affect all life on Earth? Flegal is a PhD candidate in the Department of Environmental Science, Policy, and Management at the University of California, Berkeley. Maynard is the director of the Risk Innovation Lab at Arizona State University.

As you read, consider the following questions:

1. Does researching a technology make it more likely to be used?
2. What kind of ethical considerations should geoengineers take into account during their research?
3. Should there be public debate around geoengineering?

"'Geostorm' Movie Shows Dangers of Hacking the Climate—We Need to Talk About Real-World Geoengineering Now," by Jane A. Flegal, Andrew Maynard, Academic Journalism Society, October 19, 2017. Licensed Under CC BY-ND 4.0.

Geoengineering, also called climate engineering, is a set of emerging technologies that could potentially offset some of the consequences of climate change. Some scientists are taking it seriously, considering geoengineering among the range of approaches for managing the risks of climate change—although always as a complement to, and not a substitute for, reducing emissions and adapting to the effects of climate change.

These innovations are often lumped into two categories. Carbon dioxide removal (or negative emissions) technologies set out to actively remove greenhouse gases from the atmosphere. In contrast, solar radiation management (or solar geoengineering) aims to reduce how much sunlight reaches the Earth.

Because it takes time for the climate to respond to changes, even if we stopped emitting greenhouse gases today, some level of climate change—and its associated risks—is unavoidable. Advocates of solar geoengineering argue that, if done well, these technologies might help limit some effects, including sea level rise and changes in weather patterns, and do so quickly.

But as might be expected, the idea of intentionally tinkering with the Earth's atmosphere to curb the impacts of climate change is controversial. Even conducting research into climate engineering raises some hackles.

Global Stakes Are High

Geoengineering could reshape our world in fundamental ways. Because of the global impacts that will inevitably accompany attempts to engineer the planet, this isn't a technology where some people can selectively opt in or opt out out of it: Geoengineering has the potential to affect everyone. Moreover, it raises profound questions about humans' relationship to nonhuman nature. The conversations that matter are ultimately less about the technology itself and more about what we collectively stand to gain or lose politically, culturally and socially.

Much of the debate around how advisable geoengineering research is has focused on solar geoengineering, not carbon dioxide removal. One of the worries here is that figuring out aspects of solar geoengineering could lead us down a slippery slope to actually doing it. Just doing research could make deploying solar geoengineering more likely, even if it proves to be a really bad idea. And it comes with the risk that the techniques might be bad for some while good for others, potentially exacerbating existing inequalities, or creating new ones.

For example, early studies using computer models indicated that injecting particles into the stratosphere to cool parts of Earth might disrupt the Asian and African summer monsoons, threatening the food supply for billions of people. Even if deployment wouldn't necessarily result in regional inequalities, the prospect of solar geoengineering raises questions about who has the power to shape our climate futures, and who and what gets left out.

Other concerns focus on possible unintended consequences of large-scale open-air experimentation—especially when our whole planet becomes the lab. There's a fear that the consequences would be irreversible, and that the line between research and deployment is inherently fuzzy.

And then there's the distraction problem, often known as the "moral hazard." Even researching geoengineering as one potential response to climate change may distract from the necessary and difficult work of reducing greenhouse gas levels and adapting to a changing climate—not to mention the challenges of encouraging more sustainable lifestyles and practices.

To be fair, many scientists in the small geoengineering community take these concerns very seriously. This was evident in the robust conversations around the ethics and politics of geoengineering at a recent meeting in Berlin. But there's still no consensus on whether and how to engage in responsible geoengineering research.

A Geostorm in a Teacup?

The truth is that geoengineering is still little more than a twinkle in the eyes of a small group of scientists. In the words of Jack Stilgoe, author of the book *Experiment Earth: Responsible Innovation in*

Geoengineering: "We shouldn't be scared of geoengineering, at least not yet. It is neither as exciting nor as terrifying as we have been led to believe, for the simple reason that it doesn't exist."

Compared to other emerging technologies, solar geoengineering has no industrial demand and no strong economic driver as yet, and simply doesn't appeal to national interests in global competitiveness. Because of this, it's an idea that's struggled to translate from the pages of academic papers and newsprint into reality.

Even government agencies appear wary of funding outdoor research into solar geoengineering—possibly because it's an ethically fraught area, but also because it's an academically interesting idea with no clear economic or political return for those who invest in it.

Yet some supporters make a strong case for knowing more about the potential benefits, risks and efficacy of these ideas. So scientists are beginning to turn to private funding. Harvard University, for instance, recently launched the Solar Geoengineering Research Program, funded by Bill Gates, the Hewlett Foundation and others.

As part of this program, researchers David Keith and Frank Keutsch are already planning small-scale experiments to inject fine sunlight-reflecting particles into the stratosphere above Tucson, Arizona. It's a very small experiment, and wouldn't be the first, but it aims to generate new information about whether and how such particles might one day be used to control the amount of sunlight reaching the Earth.

And importantly, it suggests that, where governments fear to tread, wealthy individuals and philanthropy may end up pushing the boundaries of geoengineering research—with or without the rest of society's consent.

The Case for Public Dialogue

The upshot is there's a growing need for public debate around whether and how to move forward.

Ultimately, no amount of scientific evidence is likely to single-handedly resolve wider debates about the benefits and risks—we've learned this much from the persistent debates about genetically modified organisms, nuclear power and other high-impact technologies.

Leaving these discussions to experts is not only counter to democratic principles but likely to be self-defeating, as more research in complex domains can often make controversies worse. The bad news here is that research on public views about geoengineering (admittedly limited to Europe and the US) suggests that most people are unfamiliar with the idea. The good news, though, is that social science research and practical experience have shown that people have the capacity to learn and deliberate on complex technologies, if given the opportunity.

As researchers in the responsible development and use of emerging technologies, we suggest less speculation about the ethics of imagined geoengineered futures, which can sometimes close down, rather than open up, decision-making about these technologies. Instead, we need more rigor in how we think about near-term choices around researching these ideas in ways that respond to social norms and contexts. This includes thinking hard about whether and how to govern privately funded research in this domain. And uncomfortable as it may feel, it means that scientists and political leaders need to remain open to the possibility that societies will not want to develop these ideas at all.

We probably won't have satellite-based weather control any time soon. But if scientists intend to research technologies to deliberately intervene in our climate system, we need to start talking seriously about whether and how to collectively, and responsibly, move forward.

Understanding Why People Support Some Methods of Geoengineering over Others

Thomas Bateman and Kieran O'Connor

In the following viewpoint, Thomas Bateman and Kieran O'Connor argue that psychology can affect the decisions we make, including which environmental policies to support. They show that when people understand the issues and technology being discussed, they are more likely to support climate mitigation and adaptation. This kind of behavioral understanding can help scientists better educate the public on the importance of their work and convince politicians to fund it. Bateman is a professor of management at the University of Virginia. O'Connor is an assistant professor of commerce at the University of Virginia.

As you read, consider the following questions:

1. Why is climate mitigation and adaptation needed?
2. Why is it important to understand the psychological roadblocks to climate mitigation?
3. How does current weather affect people's beliefs about climate change?

Conversations about climate change often derail into arguments about whether global warming exists, whether climate change is already happening, the extent to which human activity is a cause and which beliefs are based in evidence versus propaganda.

Can we have more productive discussions? We think the answer is yes, but like so many things, it depends.

Many have argued it's better to focus on strategic solutions to climate change than on science or politics or pundits. Solutions directly affect our future, whereas past-oriented debates focus on who or what is to blame and who should pay, and thus are highly polarizing.

Breaking from the old, stale debates sounds appealing, but new debates lie ahead. The solutions to our climate challenges differ from one another not just technically (cutting emissions, carbon capture, planting trees, erecting seawalls and elevating roads and buildings), but also psychologically and behaviorally.

What will be the major disagreements, and agreements, of the future? Are there different psychological and behavioral roadblocks and paths to different climate solutions, and if so, what are they? We have some initial answers to these questions, as well as important questions for going forward.

Underlying Psychologies

To begin solving the dilemmas of climate change, two primary strategic approaches require discussion: mitigation and adaptation.

For years, the primary option and a lightning rod for disagreement has been mitigation, or actions that cut the amounts of carbon and other greenhouse gases released into the atmosphere. For many, mitigation is essential; for many others, cutting emissions threatens industry, jobs, free markets and our quality of life.

Now we are entering a period of adaptation, in which we must try to reduce the impact of the coming changes. Examples include changing agricultural practices, erecting seawalls, and new approaches to architecture and living arrangements.

In some ways it is a relief to articulate ways to adapt to climate change. More coping options are better than fewer, right? Well, not necessarily. Their costs and risks differ, their effects are uncertain and varied, and decisions that will drive their deployment can derive from radically different evaluations and judgments.

We should not choose between mitigation or adaptation because we need both. We cannot lose sight of this dual need. But we will continue to face very demanding decisions about how to allocate finite resources—money, time, effort and so on—across multiple strategic options. This is where tomorrow's difficult conversations will unfold.

How will trade-offs be made, and what kinds of perceptions and biases will determine our choices? We will not be able to optimize our strategies, as objectively and effectively as humanly possible, without understanding the psychologies underlying them.

Research into the psychology of different climate solutions is in its infancy. A recent study showed how different political ideologies predict different levels of support for free market versus regulatory solutions for cutting carbon emissions.

Building on this foundation, we wanted to ascertain and test people's differing perceptions of mitigation versus adaptation as climate solutions. Such differences, we presumed, will be crucial in shaping the nature of future conversations, decisions, and actions.

In surveys of two online samples in the United States, taken when temperatures around the country differed significantly, we asked respondents to describe their beliefs about global warming and climate change. We separated and defined mitigation and adaptation strategies, and asked how much people were willing to support these different types of climate solutions.

As might be intuited, support for mitigation and for adaptation were positively correlated—people who supported one were more likely to support the other. However, while the two overlap, they do understand and perceive the two strategies to be different.

Gateway Strategy?

We found additional important differences. Overall, mitigation solutions received more support than adaptation strategies. Mitigation was also more divisive, showing the widest divide between conservatives and liberals. Adaptation was less divisive; perhaps this bodes well for future climate-solution conversations and action.

However, a key caveat is crucial for thinking about how we go forward. While we did find less disagreement around adaptation, and some general support, many people probably have not yet been exposed to information or debates about adaptation, or given it much thought.

Perhaps this novelty represents a naive stage among citizens about any issue before it becomes politicized and polarizing. On the other hand, adaptation more than mitigation is agnostic about climate-change causes; whether climate change results from human causes or natural ones is irrelevant. This may be one reason we found more agreement around adaptation.

But what will happen when adaptation is as prominent on everyone's radar as mitigation has been for years? Maybe it will become polarizing like mitigation, in which case we should have more of these conversations sooner rather than later.

Looking ahead, certain questions are crucial: As we engage in more adaptation efforts, what will we do with respect to mitigation? We cannot stop engaging in those vital activities to reduce greenhouse gases. On the other hand, the climate change train has left the station, so we have to adapt. But beware the false choice; we still have to slow the train down through more mitigation.

Theories offer competing predictions on whether engaging in adaptation will reduce our mitigation efforts. People may feel less urgency to reduce greenhouse gas emissions through mitigation if we interpret our adaptation as progress and preparedness, lessening our "felt need" to mitigate.

On the other hand, people may come to see both mitigation and adaptation as a commitment to doing all that is needed to cope with climate change, and view the two solution strategies as complementary rather than substitutes.

Ideally, adaptation is a gateway strategy for cooperation, a common ground for conversation and the beginnings of continued collaboration. Ideally, too, adaptation efforts will reveal more about the full costs of climate change. After all, action now and at the source (mitigation) is both cheaper and higher leverage than forever adapting into the future.

And now geoengineering—or deliberately altering the climate system, such as shielding the sun's heat by injecting particles into the atmosphere—is looming as a possible third solution set. Crucially, geoengineering has a different risk matrix and unstudied implications, both scientific and psychological.

Only by understanding the psychology of climate change can we deploy optimal strategies and solution mixes that vary appropriately over time and across different geographies.

Periodical and Internet Sources Bibliography

The following articles have been selected to supplement the diverse views presented in this chapter.

Brian Deese, "What Today Means for Our Global Efforts to Combat Climate Change," Medium, April 22, 2016. https://medium .com/@Deese44/what-today-means-for-our-global-efforts-to -combat-climate-change-6e225b778f1d.

Lou Del Bello, "Not All Geoengineering Is as Terrifying as You May Think," Futurism, January 1, 2018. https://futurism.com/soft -approach-geoengineering-could-help-save-planet/.

Alexia Fernandez Campbell, "Corporate America Finally Got on Board to Fight Climate Change. Then Came Trump," Vox, June 1, 2017. https://www.vox.com/2017/6/1/15724966/corporate -america-paris-climate-deal.

Stephen Fleischfresser, "Geoengineering Could Cause More Harm than Climate Change," *Cosmos*, January 23, 2018. https:// cosmosmagazine.com/technology/neering-could-cause-more -harm-than-climate-change.

Philip Fosbøl, "More Geo-engineering, Please!," ScienceNordic, January 8, 2018. http://sciencenordic.com/more-geo-engineering-please.

Bianca Nogrady, "Can Business Save the World from Climate Change?," Climate Central, August 22, 2017. http://www.climatecentral.org /news/business-corporations-climate-change-21712.

Tess Riley, "Just 100 Companies Responsible for 71% of Global Emissions, Study Says," *Guardian*, July 10, 2017. https://www .theguardian.com/sustainable-business/2017/jul/10/100-fossil -fuel-companies-investors-responsible-71-global-emissions-cdp -study-climate-change.

James Temple, "Here's the Reason We'd Never Halt a Geoengineering Project Midway Through," *MIT Technology Review*, January 22, 2018. https://www.technologyreview.com/s/610024/heres-the-reason-wed -never-halt-a-geoengineering-project-midway-through/.

Justin Worland, "The Global Plan to Combat Climate Change Faces a Reckoning," *Time*, December 20, 2017. http://time.com/5066682 /global-climate-change-plan/.

GLOBALVIEWPOINTS

CHAPTER 4

Looking to the Future

What Does Mitigation Mean?

Henry D. Jacoby and Anthony C. Janetos

In the following excerpted viewpoint, Henry D. Jacoby and Anthony C. Janetos argue that aggressive greenhouse gas emission reductions would need to be undertaken by the United States and other nations to reduce global emissions to a lower level. While they see geoengineering as a viable option, mitigation remains a top priority. Jacoby is a professor emeritus of applied economics at the Massachusetts Institute of Technology Center for Energy and Environmental Policy Research. Janetos is a professor of earth and environment at Boston University.

As you read, consider the following questions:

1. Why does climate mitigation require an understanding of Earth's natural cycles?
2. What do the impacts of greenhouse gases on the atmosphere depend on?
3. How does climate change form a self-reinforcing cycle on Earth?

Mitigation refers to actions that reduce the human contribution to the planetary greenhouse effect. Mitigation actions include lowering emissions of greenhouse gases like carbon dioxide and methane, and particles like black carbon (soot) that have a warming

"Mitigation," Jacoby, H. D., A. C. Janetos, R. Birdsey, J. Buizer, K. Calvin, F. de la Chesnaye, D. Schimel, I. Sue Wing, R. Detchon, J. Edmonds, L. Russell, and J. West, 2014: Ch. 27: Mitigation. Climate Change Impacts in the United States: The Third National Climate Assessment, J. M. Melillo, Terese (T.C.) Richmond, and G. W. Yohe, Eds., U.S. Global Change Research Program, 648-669. doi:10.7930/J0C8276J.

effect. Increasing the net uptake of carbon dioxide through land-use change and forestry can make a contribution as well. As a whole, human activities result in higher global concentrations of greenhouse gases and to a warming of the planet—and the effect is increased by various self-reinforcing cycles in the Earth system (such as the way melting sea ice results in more dark ocean water, which absorbs more heat, and leads to more sea ice loss). Also, the absorption of increased carbon dioxide by the oceans is leading to increased ocean acidity with adverse effects on marine ecosystems.

Four mitigation-related topics are assessed in this chapter. First, it presents an overview of greenhouse gas emissions and their climate influence to provide a context for discussion of mitigation efforts. Second, the chapter provides a survey of activities contributing to US emissions of carbon dioxide and other greenhouse gases. Third, it provides a summary of current government and voluntary efforts to manage these emissions. Finally, there is an assessment of the adequacy of these efforts relative to the magnitude of the climate change threat and a discussion of preparation for potential future action. While the chapter presents a brief overview of mitigation issues, it does not provide a comprehensive discussion of policy options, nor does it attempt to review or analyze the range of technologies available to reduce emissions.

[…]

Emissions, Concentrations, and Climate Forcing

Setting mitigation objectives requires knowledge of the Earth system processes that determine the relationship among emissions, atmospheric concentrations and, ultimately, climate. Human-caused climate change results mainly from the increasing atmospheric concentrations of greenhouse gases.[3] These gases cause radiative "forcing"—an imbalance of heat trapped by the atmosphere compared to an equilibrium state. Atmospheric concentrations of greenhouse gases are the result of the history of emissions and of processes that remove them from the atmosphere; for example, by "sinks" like growing forests.[4] The fraction of emissions that remains in the atmosphere, which is different for each greenhouse gas, also varies over time as a result of Earth system processes.

The impact of greenhouse gases depends partly on how long each one persists in the atmosphere.[5] Reactive gases like methane and nitrous oxide are destroyed chemically in the atmosphere, so the relationships between emissions and atmospheric concentrations are determined by the rate of those reactions. The term "lifetime" is often used to describe the speed with which a given gas is removed from the atmosphere.[6] Methane has a relatively short lifetime (largely removed within a decade or so, depending on conditions), so reductions in emissions can lead to a fairly rapid decrease in concentrations as the gas is oxidized in the atmosphere. Nitrous oxide has a much longer lifetime, taking more than 100 years to be substantially removed.[7] Other gases in this category include industrial gases, like those used as solvents and in air conditioning, some of which persist in the atmosphere for hundreds or thousands of years.

Carbon dioxide (CO_2) does not react chemically with other gases in the atmosphere, so it does not, strictly speaking, have a "lifetime."[8] Instead, the relationship between emissions and concentrations from year to year is determined by patterns of release (for example, through burning of fossil fuels) and uptake (for example, by vegetation and by the ocean).[9] Once CO_2 is emitted from any source, a portion of it is removed from the atmosphere over time by plant growth and absorption by the oceans, after which it continues to circulate in the land-atmosphere-ocean system until it is finally converted into stable forms in soils, deep ocean sediments, or other geological repositories.

Of the carbon dioxide emitted from human activities in a year, about half is removed from the atmosphere by natural processes within a century, but around 20% continues to circulate and to affect atmospheric concentrations for thousands of years.[10] Stabilizing or reducing atmospheric carbon dioxide concentrations, therefore, requires very deep reductions in future emissions—ultimately approaching zero—to compensate for past emissions that are still circulating in the Earth system. Avoiding future emissions, or capturing and storing them in stable geological storage, would prevent carbon dioxide from entering the atmosphere, and would have very long-lasting effects on atmospheric concentrations.

In addition to greenhouse gases, there can be climate effects from fine particles in the atmosphere. An example is black carbon (soot), which is released from coal burning, diesel engines, cooking fires, wood stoves, wildfires, and other combustion sources. These particles have a warming influence, especially when they absorb solar energy low in the atmosphere.[11] Other particles, such as those formed from sulfur dioxide released during coal burning, have a cooling effect by reflecting some of the sun's energy back to space or by increasing the brightness of clouds.

The effect of each gas is related to both how long it lasts in the atmosphere (the longer it lasts, the greater its influence) and its potency in trapping heat. The warming influence of different gases can be compared using "global warming potentials" (GWP), which combine these two effects, usually added up over a 100-year time period. Global warming potentials are referenced to carbon dioxide—which is defined as having a GWP of 1.0—and the combined effect of multiple gases is denoted in carbon dioxide equivalents, or CO_2-e.

The relationship between emissions and concentrations of gases can be modeled using Earth System Models.[12] Such models apply our understanding of biogeochemical processes that remove greenhouse gas from the atmosphere to predict their future concentrations. These models show that stabilizing CO_2 emissions would not stabilize its atmospheric concentrations but instead result in a concentration that would increase at a relatively steady rate. Stabilizing atmospheric concentrations of CO_2 would require reducing emissions far below present-day levels. Concentration and emissions scenarios, such as the recently developed Representative Concentration Pathways (RCPs) and scenarios developed earlier by the Intergovernmental Panel on Climate Change's (IPCC) Special

Report on Emissions Scenarios (SRES), are used in Earth System Models to study potential future climates. The RCPs span a range of atmospheric targets for use by climate modelers,[13,14] as do the SRES cases. These global analyses form a framework within which the climate contribution of US mitigation efforts can be assessed. In this report, special attention is given to the SRES A2 scenario (similar to RCP 8.5), which assumes continued increases in emissions, and the SRES B1 scenario (close to RCP 4.5), which assumes a substantial reduction of emissions.

Geoengineering

Geoengineering has been proposed as a third option for addressing climate change in addition to, or alongside, mitigation and adaptation. Geoengineering refers to intentional modifications of the Earth system as a means to address climate change. Three types of activities have been proposed: 1) carbon dioxide removal (CDR), which boosts CO_2 removal from the atmosphere by various means, such as fertilizing ocean processes and promoting land-use practices that help take up carbon, 2) solar radiation management (SRM), which reflects a small percentage of sunlight back into space to offset warming from greenhouse gases,[15] and 3) direct capture and storage of CO_2 from the atmosphere.[16]

Current research suggests that SRM or CDR could diminish the impacts of climate change. However, once undertaken, sudden cessation of SRM would exacerbate the climate effects on human populations and ecosystems, and some CDR might interfere with oceanic and terrestrial ecosystem processes.[17] SRM undertaken by itself would not slow increases in atmospheric CO_2 concentrations, and would therefore also fail to address ocean acidification. Furthermore, existing international institutions are not adequate to manage such global interventions. The risks associated with such purposeful perturbations to the Earth system are thus poorly understood, suggesting the need for caution and comprehensive research, including consideration of the implicit moral hazards.[18]

Notes

3. IPCC, 2007: *Climate Change 2007: The Physical Science Basis. Contribution of Working Group I to the Fourth Assessment Report of the Intergovernmental Panel on Climate Change.* S. Solomon, D. Qin, M. Manning, Z. Chen, M. Marquis, K. B. Averyt, M. Tignor, and H. L. Miller, Eds. Cambridge University Press, 996 pp. [Available online at http://www.ipcc.ch/publications_and_data/publications_ipcc_fourth _assessment_report_wg1_report_the_physical_science_basis.htm]

4. Plattner, G. K., R. Knutti, F. Joos, T. F. Stocker, W. von Bloh, V. Brovkin, D. Cameron, E. Driesschaert, S. Dutkiewicz, M. Eby, N. R. Edwards, T. Fichefet, J. C. Hargreaves, C. D. Jones, M. F. Loutre, H. D. Matthews, A. Mouchet, S. A. Müller, S. Nawrath, A. Price, A. Sokolov, K. M. Strassmann, and A. J. Weaver, 2008: Long-term climate commitments projected with climate-carbon cycle models. *Journal of Climate*, **21**, 2721-2751, doi:10.1175/2007jcli1905.1. [Available online at http://journals. ametsoc.org/doi/pdf/10.1175/2007JCLI1905.1]

5. Denman, K. L., G. Brasseur, A. Chidthaisong, P. Ciais, P. M. Cox, R. E. Dickinson, D. Hauglustaine, C. Heinze, E. Holland, D. Jacob, U. Lohmann, S. Ramachandran, P. L. da Silva Dias, S. C. Wofsy, and X. Zhang, 2007: Ch. 7: Couplings between changes in the climate system and biogeochemistry. *Climate Change 2007: The Physical Science Basis. Contribution of Working Group I to the Fourth Assessment Report of the Intergovernmental Panel on Climate Change*, S. Solomon, D. Qin, M. Manning, Z. Chen, M. Marquis, K. B. Averyt, M. Tignor, and H. L. Miller, Eds., Cambridge University Press, 499-587. [Available online at http://www.ipcc.ch/pdf /assessment-report/ar4/wg1/ar4-wg1-chapter7.pdf]

6. Cicerone, R. J., and R. S. Oremland, 1988: Biogeochemical aspects of atmospheric methane. *Global Biogeochemical Cycles*, **2**, 299-327, doi:10.1029/ GB002i004p00299.

7. IPCC, 1995: *The Science of Climate Change. Contribution of Working Group I to the Second Assessment Report of the Intergovernmental Panel on Climate Change. Summary for Policymakers and Technical Summary.* Cambridge University Press.

8. Moore, B., III, and B. H. Braswell, 1994: The lifetime of excess atmospheric carbon dioxide. *Global Biogeochemical Cycles*, **8**, 23-38, doi:10.1029/93GB03392.

9. Schimel, D. S., 1995: Terrestrial ecosystems and the carbon cycle. *Global Change Biology*, 1, 77-91, doi:10.1111/j.1365-2486.1995.tb00008.x.

10. GCP, 2010: Ten Years of Advancing Knowledge on the Global Carbon Cycle and Its Management. L. Poruschi, S. Dhakal, and J. Canadel, Eds., Global Carbon Project, Tsukuba, Japan. [Available online at http://www.globalcarbonproject.org/global /pdf/GCP_10years_med_res.pdf]

——: Carbon Budget 2012: An Annual Update of the Global Carbon Budget and Trends. Global Carbon Project. [Available online at http://www.globalcarbonproject.org /carbonbudget/]

11. Archer, D., 2010: *The Global Carbon Cycle.* Princeton University Press, 205 pp.

12. Grieshop, A. P., C. C. O. Reynolds, M. Kandlikar, and H. Dowlatabadi, 2009: A black-carbon mitigation wedge. *Nature Geoscience*, **2**, 533-534, doi:10.1038/ngeo595.

13. Moss, R. H., J. A. Edmonds, K. A. Hibbard, M. R. Manning, S. K. Rose, D. P. van Vuuren, T. R. Carter, S. Emori, M. Kainuma, T. Kram, G. A. Meehl, J. F. B. Mitchell, N. Nakicenovic, K. Riahi, S. J. Smith, R. J. Stouffer, A. M. Thomson, J. P. Weyant, and T. J. Willbanks, 2010: The next generation of scenarios for climate change research and assessment. *Nature*, **463**, 747-756, doi:10.1038/nature08823.

14. van Vuuren, D. P., J. Cofala, H. E. Eerens, R. Oostenrijk, C. Heyes, Z. Klimont, M. G. J. Den Elzen, and M. Amann, 2006: Exploring the ancillary benefits of the Kyoto

Protocol for air pollution in Europe. *Energy Policy*, **34**, 444-460, doi:10.1016/j. enpol.2004.06.012.

15. Shepherd, J. G., 2009: *Geoengineering the Climate: Science, Governance and Uncertainty*. Royal Society, 82 pp. [Available online at http://eprints.soton. ac.uk/156647/1/Geoengineering_the_climate.pdf]

16. American Physical Society, 2011: Direct Air Capture of CO_2 with Chemicals: A Technology Assessment for the APS Panel on Public Affairs, 100 pp., American Physical Society. [Available online at http://www.aps.org/policy/reports /assessments/upload/dac2011.pdf]

17. Russell, L. M., P. J. Rasch, G. M. Mace, R. B. Jackson, J. Shepherd, P. Liss, M. Leinen, D. Schimel, N. E. Vaughan, A. C. Janetos, P. W. Boyd, R. J. Norby, K. Caldeira, J. Merikanto, P. Artaxo, J. Melillo, and M. G. Morgan, 2012: Ecosystem impacts of geoengineering: A review for developing a science plan. *AMBIO: A Journal of the Human Environment*, **41**, 350-369, doi:10.1007/s13280-012-0258-5. [Available online at http://www.bz.duke.edu/jackson/ambio2012.pdf]

18. Parson, E. A., and D. W. Keith, 2013: End the deadlock on governance of geoengineering research. *Science*, **339**, 1278-1279, doi:10.1126/science.1232527.

The Paris Agreement Is a Key to the Solution

David Waskow and Jennifer Morgan

In the following viewpoint, David Waskow and Jennifer Morgan argue that the 2015 Paris Agreement marked a turning point in global action on climate change. The 1992 United Nations Framework Convention on Climate Change (UNFCCC) is an international environmental treaty created to stabilize the amount of greenhouse gas in the atmosphere at a level that prevents dangerous human interference with the climate system. In 2015, the UNFCCC adopted the Paris Agreement, wherein each participating country would attempt to mitigate climate change enough to keep the global temperature from rising more than 2 degrees Celsius. Each country determines its own plan and regularly reports on its efforts and results. Some have criticized the agreement for not doing more to fight climate change and for having no real enforcement mechanism. Waskow is director of the World Resources Institute's International Climate Initiative. Morgan is the former director of the World Resources Institute.

As you read, consider the following questions:

1. Why is transparency an important part of the Paris Agreement?
2. What are the long-term goals of the Paris Agreement?
3. What is the purpose of meeting every five years?

"The Paris Agreement: Turning Point for a Climate Solution," by David Waskow and Jennifer Morgan, World Resources Institute, December 12, 2015. http://www.wri.org/blog/2015/12/paris-agreement-turning-point-climate-solution Licensed under CC by 4.0 International.

Today marks an historic turning point in global action on climate change. At the UN Climate Conference in Paris, known as COP21, 196 countries joined together in the Paris Agreement, a universal pact that sets the world on a course to a zero-carbon, resilient, prosperous and fair future. While the Agreement is not enough by itself to solve the problem, it places us clearly on the path to a truly global solution.

Building on the foundation of national climate plans from 187 countries, the Paris Agreement is a reflection of the remarkable momentum from cities, companies, civil society groups and others that complement the global will to act that has grown over the years since the first international conference on climate change in 1992.

The Paris Agreement will maintain and accelerate that momentum. It offers clear direction with:

- long-term goals and signals,

- a commitment to return regularly to make climate action stronger,

- a response to the impact of extreme climate events on the most vulnerable,

- the transparency needed to ensure action takes place and

- finance, capacity building and technology to enable real change.

But the Agreement does even more: it marks a new type of international cooperation where developed and developing countries are united in a common framework, and all are involved, engaged contributors. It reflects the growing recognition that climate action offers tremendous opportunities and benefits, and that climate impacts can be tackled effectively, with the unity of purpose that has brought us to this moment.

The moment in Paris extended far beyond the Agreement itself. Cities and forests, business and finance—all these were part of the many initiatives and commitments that were launched or strengthened over the past two weeks. And they will be key to the solution as action moves forward with the energy generated by Paris.

Key Provisions

Long-Term Mitigation Goals

The Paris Agreement sets landmark goals for taking action on climate change, aiming to keep temperature rise to well below 2 degrees C (3.6 degrees F) and to pursue efforts to keep it to limit temperature increase to 1.5 degrees C (2.7 degrees F). To achieve this, countries will aim to peak global emissions as soon as possible and—remarkably—countries agreed to reduce emissions rapidly to reach net-zero greenhouse gas (GHG) emissions in the second half of the century. They will do that taking equity, sustainable development and poverty into account.

Five-Year Cycles of Action

To build on the momentum from countries' national climate plans put forward for Paris, countries have agreed to a process to ramp up action on emissions every five years. By 2020, countries have agreed to come back and either submit new or updated national climate plans (known as nationally determined contributions). Every five years after that, countries will submit new contributions. Countries have also agreed that their mitigation plans will represent a progression beyond their previous efforts.

Five-Year Comprehensive Global Stocktake

The Agreement establishes a strong process for countries to regularly assess implementation and take stock of climate action every five years, called the Global Stocktake. This will assess implementation of action on mitigation, adaptation and support, including finance, and inform implementation of countries' climate plans. Assessment will start in 2023, but countries have agreed to return in 2018 to review implementation of mitigation measures to inform their 2020 mitigation contributions.

Adaptation

Adaptation to climate change is a central issue for global climate action in this Agreement, where it is on par with mitigation. It establishes a global goal of enhancing adaptive capacity, strengthening resilience and reducing vulnerability, including an adequate adaptation response given the Agreement's temperature goal. The Agreement creates a cycle of action for strengthening adaptation efforts regularly, similar to the mitigation cycle. Countries will have flexibility on the timing and methods for communicating information about their adaptation activities or efforts. Support will be provided to developing countries for planning, implementation and communication of adaptation activities.

Loss and Damage

The Agreement addresses the important issue of loss and damage, referring to the serious impacts of climate change when mitigation and adaptation fail. Those people who are affected by climate change may face damage to their property or health, or in worse cases, permanent loss of land or livelihoods, or even loss of life. The Agreement acknowledges the issue of loss and damage as separate from adaptation, and makes permanent the Warsaw International Mechanism (WIM) on Loss and Damage, established two years ago [2013] to find ways to address these issues. The outcome also establishes a task force on climate change-related displacement within the WIM, and makes clear that the loss and damage provision does not create new legal liability for emitting countries.

Finance

Finance will provide the needed power to turn the world toward a zero-carbon, climate-resilient future, and the purpose of the Agreement states that all financial flows—both public and private— need to be shifted from high to low emissions activities and risky to resilient investments. The Agreement makes clear that developed countries will continue to provide and mobilize finance to support developing countries, and developed countries agreed to continue their 2020 commitment of mobilizing $100 billion a year until 2025. For the period after that, governments will adopt a new, higher, collective goal, though the extent to which finance will increase, and who will mobilize it, is a significant outstanding question. The Agreement opens the door for developing countries to provide support to their peers, recognizing that some developing countries are already doing so.

In addition, governments agreed to balance public funding between adaptation and mitigation, and agreed to significantly increase support for adaptation before 2020, which is of vital importance for the most vulnerable countries dealing with the impacts of a warmer world. Countries also committed to improve reporting on finance, with everyone providing information about finance provided or received, as appropriate.

Transparency

The Agreement establishes a common system for transparency for all countries. Through an enhanced transparency framework all countries will be required to report on their emissions and track progress on achieving their nationally determined contributions regularly. The information provided by all parties will be subject to an expert review and facilitative multilateral consideration of progress. The framework provides flexibility and support that takes account of different countries' capacities. Developed countries will report on the finance and support they provide, and developing countries will report on the finance and support needed and received.

Capacity Building

For the new international climate agreement to be universal, countries acknowledged that effective capacity building is vital to enable developing countries to take strong climate action. To elevate this issue, countries established the new Paris Committee on Capacity Building to oversee a work plan to enhance capacity building. The Committee will identify capacity gaps and needs, foster international cooperation and identify opportunities to strengthen capacity for climate action.

Legal Form

The Paris Agreement is a universal, legal agreement under the UNFCCC, with the participation of all countries. It will be open for signature next April, and will come into force in January 2020. Notably, the Agreement contains a strong, legally binding framework for reporting, transparency and review of implementation capable of driving greater ambition to tackle climate change. The establishment of a mechanism to facilitate implementation and promote compliance will provide further assurance of Parties' actions.

Climate Conference Highlights

COP21's outcome fulfilled the promise of its opening day, when more than 150 heads of state and government converged in Paris to express their commitment to climate action and a viable agreement. On the same day, 20 countries and 27 representatives from the private sector announced a multi-billion dollar clean energy fund and commitment to increase R&D investments, a major boost to the talks. This set the stage for more progress on climate action across a wide spectrum of areas.

Forests and Restoration

Opening day, November 30, also saw significant government commitments to protect forests, including $5 billion in funding from Germany, Norway and the United Kingdom. Global Forest Watch Climate, launched during the conference, offers the potential to shift the debate on monitoring forest-based emissions. The African Forest and Landscapes Restoration Initiative (AFR100) seeks to restore 100 million hectares (nearly 250 million acres) of degraded and deforested land in Africa by 2030. Initiative 20x20 is landscape restoration effort in Latin America and the Caribbean that has now reached nearly 28 million hectares (nearly 70 million acres) and $730 million in investment.

Cities

Building efficiency, sustainable mobility and interactive tools were among the city-level solutions advanced to prevent carbon-intensive congestion, sprawl and inefficiencies from locking in for decades to come. WRI announced 25 new partners to the Building Efficiency Accelerator as part of the UN SE4All initiative and presented the New Climate Economy message of better transport, better climate. A coalition including WRI advanced the Paris Process on Mobility and Climate to position mitigation and adaptation contributions from transport sector. Along with UK DECC, WRI demonstrated the 2050 Global Calculator, an interactive model—WRI contributed the transport section—that allows users to explore 2 degrees C pathways. Looking ahead, the UN announced the Climate Action 2016 conference to deepen and expand action in six focus areas—with cities and transport being key.

Business

More than 114 companies committed to set emissions reduction targets in line with Science Based Targets, using what scientists say is necessary to keep global warming below 2 degrees C. Participating companies have combined annual carbon dioxide emissions equivalent to what 125 coal-fired power plants emit in a year. Goldman Sachs announced plans to invest $150 billion in clean energy projects and technology. The investment bank previously had a target to invest $40 billion in clean energy technologies by 2012, and will now almost quadruple that by 2025. Google added 842 megawatts of renewable energy capacity around the world, nearly doubling the amount of renewables it has purchased to 2 gigawatts, equivalent to taking nearly 1 million cars off the road.

Investment

Institutional investors and banks signaled their plans to build climate change considerations into their decisions. Allianz and ABP officially joined the Portfolio Carbon Initiative, bringing the value of the Coalition's assets under management to $600 billion.

Five Principles for Mainstreaming Climate Action within Financial Institutions also launched, with more than two dozen financial institutions indicating their intent to incorporate climate change into strategies and operations. An alliance of global investors, development banks, financial sector associations and NGOs [nongovernmental organizations] launched the Green Infrastructure Investment Coalition to support the accelerated financing of green infrastructure through investor-government global and regional dialogues, and 27 global investors issued the Paris Green Bonds Statement to support policies that drive the development of long term, sustainable global markets in green bonds.

People Are More Comfortable Supporting "Natural" Forms of Geoengineering

Anita Talberg and Tim Flannery

In the following viewpoint, Anita Talberg and Tim Flannery argue that reducing greenhouse gas emissions alone will not solve the climate change crisis. Some types of geoengineering, like solar radiation management, are seen as unnatural. As the authors point out, people are more likely to support geoengineering when it's considered "natural," regardless of the science behind it. These kinds of beliefs can affect which technologies are funded and supported. Talberg is a PhD student in the Australian-German Climate and Energy College at the University of Melbourne. Flannery is chief commissioner at the Climate Commission.

As you read, consider the following questions:

1. Who should get to approve scientific research that can impact the whole planet?
2. Why is reducing greenhouse gas emissions not enough to help stabilize the climate?
3. What types of geoengineering are seen as natural?

N o matter how much we reduce greenhouse gas emissions, it will not be enough to keep global warming below 2C—the internationally agreed "safe" limit. This fact has been implied by the Intergovernmental Panel on Climate Change, and confirmed again recently by international research.

Does this mean we should give up? Not at all. There is a plan B to keep warming below dangerous levels: helping the planet to take more carbon dioxide out of the atmosphere.

In his new book *Atmosphere of Hope*, Tim Flannery, Climate Councillor and Professorial Fellow at the Melbourne Sustainable Society Institute (and co-author of this article), argues that these strategies will be necessary to combat climate change, but cannot substitute completely for reducing emissions.

Plan B

When the term "plan B" is mentioned in relation to climate change, ideas immediately turn to the presumed "techno-fix" of geoengineering.

Geoengineering, or "climate engineering" as it is also known, is a broad, all-encompassing definition that includes both managing solar radiation and removing carbon dioxide from the atmosphere.

Solar radiation management techniques are those that change the balance of the sun's energy reaching the Earth, versus the amount being reflected out. Like deploying a parasol, this aims to cool the planet without adjusting greenhouse gas levels.

In contrast, carbon dioxide removal methods "suck" carbon dioxide from the atmosphere to store it semi-permanently either underground, in rocks, or in animals, plants and ecosystems.

Often the distinctions between these two methods (and their potential impacts and different governance challenges) are not made clear. It is not uncommon for the term "geoengineering" to be used only to refer to managing the sun's radiation reaching the Earth. This is presumably why at the first international conference on climate engineering in 2014 the chair Mark Lawrence called on all delegates to be discerning and precise in their use of language.

Talk of geoengineering tends to elicit uncomfortable feelings. This is in part because it has no obvious governance—how do you decide who takes action that will affect the whole world?

It is also because many of the techniques under the geoengineering umbrella have potentially serious adverse side-effects, both environmental and social (like a cure that could be worse than the disease). It is also largely because it feels wrong, conceptually, to try to address a problem caused by the dominance of Man over Nature through the further dominance of Man over Nature.

The Third Way

If emissions reduction is not enough and geoengineering ideas are decried as "ludicrous Bond-villain style schemes," there must be another way ... and there is.

According to research from the Tyndall Centre for Climate Change Research, geoengineering methods that are perceived as "natural" are more likely to receive public support.

What this suggests is that humanity would be more accepting of new proposals to deal with climate change if they worked alongside natural processes. "Natural" options would be ones that strengthened and supported the environment in doing what it already does: processing excess atmospheric carbon dioxide. This is the third way to deal with climate change.

The analogy has been drawn to a person battling weight gain. Reducing calorie intake is important but this should be supplemented by exercise to help the body do what it already does: burn excess fat. This analogy also likens some geoengineering techniques to lap-band surgery.

Testing Geoengineering Outside the Lab

In response to the threat posed by global climate change, most nations have committed to significant mitigation efforts, through the Paris Agreement, to reduce greenhouse gas emissions. Countries are also aggressively working on climate change adaptation to restore wetlands, erect seawalls and build local resilience to the effects of global warming.

But will these collective efforts be enough? Some scientists are trying another approach, exploring new tools to deliberately alter the global climate system. These discrete and diverse technologies are often grouped under the all-encompassing and poorly defined rubric of "climate engineering" or "geoengineering." These radically different approaches, which are in various stages of development, aim to either halt the process of global warming by removing greenhouse gases from the atmosphere or to counteract warming already under way.

The problem is, while several tools seem to be gaining traction in computer models, laboratories, and even real-world experiments, public discourse has not kept pace with their advancement. To date, there has been too little transparency and international dialogue around the progress, feasibility, risks and benefits of these efforts. Documenting and tracking the array of tools in development is crucial for understanding their full impact, debating their implementation, and safeguarding their appropriate use. The public will need transparency and discourse before these methods could gain acceptance and be considered for wide-scale adoption.

Climate engineering and current mitigation and adaptation efforts are not mutually exclusive. Experts generally agree that these new technological approaches alone are unlikely to provide adequate protection from the dangers posed by rising global temperatures. It will be important to compare technologies and assess how they best fit with climate actions already underway. This will require input from the wider scientific community, social scientists, policymakers, lawyers, ethicists, nongovernmental organizations and citizens. Broad expertise is needed to anticipate, prevent and moderate the possible unintended consequences of these systems for our natural, social, political and economic systems.

There are real risks to opting into—or out of—climate engineering. While it is tempting to simply be categorically for or against climate engineering, decision-makers are at a crossroads where it is more critical— and more responsible—to gather scientific facts and ask as many questions as possible about what the deployment of these technologies might mean for individuals, societies, nations and regions. As technologies advance, those who deploy them will need to respect political borders, protect the global commons, and abide by cultural norms.

"Could Geoengineering Save the Planet from Global Warming?," by Deborah Gordon, David Livingston, Carnegie Endowment for International Peace, September 21, 2017.

The third way is thus a concept that is described in *Atmosphere of Hope* as:

encompassing proposals and experiments that shed light on how Earth's natural system for maintaining the carbon balance might be stimulated to draw CO_2 out of the air and sea at a faster rate than occurs presently, and how we might store the recovered CO_2 safely.

In essence, the division between the third way and geoengineering is a functional one.

Third-way ideas are extremely varied. They include planting trees or building artificial trees that capture CO_2 from the air; producing and using biochar; farming CO_2-absorbing seaweed; and constructing buildings from carbon-neutral cement capable of capturing CO_2 from the air.

Determining whether a particular idea aligns with the third-way concept needs to be done on a case-by-case basis.

Ocean fertilisation is a good example. It involves adding elements or compounds (such as iron, nitrogen, phosphate, silica, or urea) to the oceans in an area that is nutrient deficient. This stimulates biological growth that can absorb carbon through photosynthesis.

Although the concept builds on existing natural processes, the outcome is uncertain and research suggests that there are environmental risks such as damaging fisheries and marine biodiversity, causing localised warming, altering cloud formations and maybe even increasing greenhouse gas emissions.

Given the current state of research, ocean fertilisation does not look feasible or appropriate and thus may not qualify as third-way (despite sitting squarely under the geoengineering umbrella).

Direct Action Could Do the Job

The third way may be easier for us to grapple with than geoengineering. This is perhaps because the third-way concept is already partially embedded in the Australian government's approach to climate policy.

The government's Direct Action mechanism is aimed at providing incentives for tackling rising atmospheric greenhouse gases. The Minister for the Environment has called Direct Action "source blind as to the type of abatement." That means that the policy instrument does not discriminate on the technology or the sector within which the abatement takes place.

Direct Action also does not discriminate between emissions reduction and emissions removal (despite being financed by a government purse known as the Emissions Reduction Fund). In fact, the long title of the legislation is "An Act about projects to remove carbon dioxide from the atmosphere and projects to avoid emissions of greenhouse gases, and for other purposes."

Of the 30 or so methods currently available for funding under the Emissions Reduction Fund only a small handful could be classified as third-way. And at this stage they are all within the agriculture and forestry sector.

This is because the legislation for Direct Action is inherited from the previous government's Carbon Farming Initiative that focused exclusively on the land sector. However, technically (if not economically) there is the potential for third-way methods to gain more importance under Direct Action.

The Third-Way Cannot Be the Only Way

What should not be ignored, however, is the fact that the total capacity for third-way methods to help meet the climate change challenge is limited by a number of factors, including by nature itself, but also the pace of innovation and funding.

In *Atmosphere of Hope*, it is estimated that by mid-century up to about 40% of current global emissions could potentially be absorbed in this way.

Globally emissions from the burning [of] fossil fuels and from cement production continue to increase.

In Australia, emissions from the combustion of fossil fuels levelled off in 2009, and even started to decrease (from reduced electricity demand) but have started to increase again in the latest financial year. The third way can only be a supplement to serious emissions reduction in Australia and worldwide, it should not be seen as a substitute.

Geoengineering Is Everyone's Business

Rob Bellamy

In the following viewpoint, Rob Bellamy argues for the need for geoengineering while measuring it against the public's legitimate concern about the safety of such research. Like others, Bellamy discusses the difficulty that comes in legislating something which can have global effects. He believes that the public requires more involvement in the scientific community's debate about the use of geoengineering. More research needs to be done into finding the right balance between furthering scientific discovery and safety. Bellamy is a James Martin Research Fellow in the Institute for Science, Innovation and Society at the University of Oxford. He researches the interactions between climate change and society.

As you read, consider the following questions:

1. What is the danger of the termination problem?
2. What are the four principal concerns the public has with geoengineering?
3. Why should scientists take the views of the public into account?

"Why You Need to Get Involved in the Geoengineering Debate—Now," by Rob Bellamy, Academic Journalism Society, October 19, 2017. https://theconversation.com/why-you-need-to-get-involved-in-the-geoengineering-debate-now-85619 Licensed Under CC BY-ND 4.0.

The prospect of engineering the world's climate system to tackle global warming is becoming more and more likely. This may seem like a crazy idea but I, and over 250 other scientists, policy makers and stakeholders from around the globe recently descended on Berlin to debate the promises and perils of geoengineering.

There are many touted methods of engineering the climate. Early, outlandish ideas included installing a "space sunshade": a massive mirror orbiting the Earth to reflect sunlight. The ideas most in discussion now may not seem much more realistic—spraying particles into the stratosphere to reflect sunlight, or fertilising the oceans with iron to encourage algal growth and carbon dioxide sequestration through photosynthesis.

But the prospect of geoengineering has become a lot more real since the Paris Agreement. The 2015 Paris Agreement set out near universal, legally binding commitments to keep the increase in global temperature to well below 2°C above pre-industrial levels and even to aim for limiting the rise to 1.5°C. The Intergovernmental Panel on Climate Change (IPCC) has concluded that meeting these targets is possible—but nearly all of their scenarios rely on the extensive deployment of some form of geoengineering by the end of the century.

How to Engineer the Climate

Geoengineering comes in two distinct flavours. The first is greenhouse gas removal: those ideas that would seek to remove and store carbon dioxide and other greenhouse gases from the atmosphere. The second is solar radiation management: the ideas that would seek to reflect a level of sunlight away from the Earth.

Solar radiation management is the more controversial of the two, doing nothing to address the root cause of climate change—greenhouse gas emissions—and raising a whole load of concerns about undesirable side effects, such as changes to regional weather patterns. And then there is the so-called "termination problem." If we ever stopped engineering the climate in this way then global temperature would abruptly bounce back to where it would have been without it. And if we had not been reducing or removing emissions at the same time, this could be a very sharp and sudden rise indeed.

Most climate models that see the ambitions of the Paris Agreement achieved assume the use of greenhouse gas removal, particularly bio-energy coupled with carbon capture and storage technology. But, as the recent conference revealed, although research in the field is steadily gaining ground, there is also a dangerous gap between its current state of the art and the achievability of the Paris Agreement on climate change.

The Paris Agreement—and its implicit dependence on greenhouse gas removal—has undoubtedly been one of the most significant developments to impact on the field of geoengineering since the last conference of its kind back in 2014. This shifted the emphasis of the conference away from the more controversial and attention-grabbing solar radiation management and towards the more mundane but policy relevant greenhouse gas removal.

Controversial Experiments

But there were moments when sunlight reflecting methods still stole the show. A centrepiece of the conference was the solar radiation management experiments campfire, where David Keith and his colleagues from the Harvard University Solar Geoengineering Research Programme laid out their experimental plans. They aim to lift an instrument package to a height of 20km using a high-altitude balloon and release a small amount of reflective particles into the atmosphere.

This would not be the first geoengineering experiment. Scientists, engineers and entrepreneurs have already begun experimenting with various ideas, several of which have attracted a great degree of public interest and controversy. A particularly notable case was one UK project, in which plans to release a small amount of water into the atmosphere at a height of 1km using a pipe tethered to a balloon were cancelled in 2013 owing to concerns over intellectual property.

Such experiments will be essential if geoengineering ideas are to ever become technically viable contributors to achieving the goals of the Paris Agreement. But it is the governance of experiments, not their technical credentials, that has always been and still remains the most contentious area of the geoengineering debate.

Critics warned that the Harvard experiment could be the first step on a "slippery slope" towards an undesirable deployment and therefore must be restrained. But advocates argued that the technology needs to be developed before we can know what it is that we are trying to govern.

The challenge for governance is not to back either one of these extremes, but rather to navigate a responsible path between them.

How to Govern?

The key to defining a responsible way to govern geoengineering experiments is accounting for public interests and concerns. Would-be geoengineering experimenters, including those at Harvard, routinely try to account for these concerns by appealing to their experiments being of a small scale and a limited extent. But, as I argued in the conference, in public discussions on the scale and extent of geoengineering experiments their meaning has been subjective and always qualified by other concerns.

My colleagues and I have found that the public have at least four principal concerns about geoengineering experiments: their level of containment; uncertainty around what the outcomes would be; the reversibility of any impacts, and the intent behind them. A small scale experiment unfolding indoors might therefore be deemed unacceptable if it raised concerns about private interests, for example. On the other hand, a large scale experiment conducted outdoors could be deemed acceptable if it did not release materials into the open environment.

How NASA Responds to Climate Change

NASA, with its Eyes on the Earth and wealth of knowledge on the Earth's climate system and its components, is one of the world's experts in climate science. NASA's purview is to provide the robust scientific data needed to understand climate change. For example, data from the agency's Gravity Recovery and Climate Experiment (GRACE) and Ice, Cloud and land Elevation Satellite (ICESat) missions and from radar instruments in space have shown rapid changes in the Earth's great ice sheets. The Jason-3, Jason-2/OSTM Surface Topography Mission (OSTM) and Jason-1 missions have documented an increasing sea level since 1992.

NASA makes detailed climate data available to the global community—the public, policy- and decision-makers and scientific and planning agencies around the world. It is not NASA's role to set climate policy or prescribe particular responses or solutions to climate change.

Started in 2010, NASA's Carbon Monitoring System (CMS) is a forward-looking initiative established under direction by the US government. The CMS is improving the monitoring of global carbon stocks (where carbon is stored around the planet) and fluxes (how carbon is cycled from one stock to the next). The ultimate goal is to make breakthroughs in quantifying, understanding and predicting how worldwide carbon sources and sinks are changing, since this could have major ramifications for how our planet will respond to increasing emissions and/or efforts to combat climate change. The work will also help inform near-term policy development and planning.

NASA's related Megacities Carbon Project is focused on the problem of accurately measuring and monitoring greenhouse-gas emissions from the world's biggest cities. About three-quarters of fossil-fuel carbon dioxide emissions come from about 2 percent of the land surface—the cities and the power plants that feed them. At present the focus is on pilot projects in Los Angeles and Paris that sample the air there. The goal is to add other cities around the world and to ultimately deploy a worldwide urban carbon monitoring system that will enable local policymakers to fully account for the many sources and sinks of carbon and how they change over time.

> Although NASA's main focus is not on energy-technology research and development, work is being done around the agency and by/with various partners and collaborators to find viable alternative sources of energy to power our needs. These sources of energy include the wind, waves, the sun and biofuels.
>
> *"Responding to Climate Change,"* National Aeronautics and Space Administration.

Under certain conditions the four dimensions could be aligned. The challenge for governance is to account for these—and likely other—dimensions of perceived controllability. This means that public involvement in the design of governance itself needs to be front and centre in the development of geoengineering experiments.

A whole range of two-way dialogue methods are available—focus groups, citizens juries, deliberative workshops and many others. And to those outside of formal involvement in such processes—read about geoengineering, talk about geoengineering. We need to start a society-wide conversation on how to govern such controversial technologies.

Public interests and concerns need to be drawn out well in advance of an experiment and the results used to meaningfully shape how we govern it. This will not only make the the experiment more legitimate, but also make it substantively better.

Make no mistake, experiments will be needed if we are to learn the worth of geoengineering ideas. But they must be done with public values at their core.

The Potential Benefits of Geoengineering Are Too Great to Not Cooperate

David A. Dana

In the following viewpoint, David A. Dana describes some of the potential effects of the United States's withdrawal from the Paris Agreement. Along with damaging the environment, he argues, it could encourage other nations to leave the agreement. Dana believes that when it comes to climate change, nations and scientists must cooperate. The Paris Agreement is a sign that the world is finally beginning to take the threat of climate change seriously. Geoengineering will require global cooperation if it is to be undertaken in an ethical manner. The Paris Agreement offered a good start for how nations can begin to work together. Dana is a law professor at Northwestern University with a concentration on energy and environmental law and policy.

As you read, consider the following questions:

1. Why does the United States leaving the Paris Agreement weaken its power?
2. How could SRM technology be weaponized?
3. Why is SRM so popular despite the potential risks?

The Trump administration's decision to withdraw from the Paris Agreement has invoked condemnation and consternation from many commentators, including many of the United States' strongest allies.

While the withdrawal undoubtedly will impede efforts to reduce global greenhouse gas emissions—and very regrettably so—it may have a negative effect on another area of global climate negotiation: geoengineering.

Geoengineering, in the form of deflecting the sun's energy, has been discussed as a technologically feasible, yet highly risky, near-term response to the rapid warming of the planet. The only reasonable, and indeed sane, way for the debate over the contentious question of geoengineering to proceed is in the context of inclusive, transparent, reasoned international cooperation—the same process that led to the Paris Agreement.

Yet the [President Donald] Trump withdrawal has weakened the very institution that could be the most viable nexus for such international cooperation.

What's Inside Paris Accord

Mitigating the effects of climate change by lowering greenhouse gas levels is the primary focus of the Paris Agreement, which is built on voluntary commitments by each member state to lower greenhouse gas emissions. The Trump administration's withdrawal—and more generally, its rejection of the [President Barack] Obama-era efforts to cut emissions via the Clean Power Plan—may lead other countries to back away from their commitments.

But climate change mitigation is only part of the needed global response to climate change in the coming decades. There also is a need for global cooperation with respect to both climate change adaptation and geoengineering. The agreement could foster such cooperation, but again, only if nations do not defect.

Like climate mitigation, the need to adapt to climate change is explicitly built into the Paris Agreement. The accord calls for the transfer of resources from wealthy countries to poor countries that will face the harshest effects from changes to the climate which are already baked in and by now are unavoidable. These funds are meant to strengthen the adaptive capacity of poor countries.

Weak adaptive capacity increases the chances that climate effects, such as epidemics, population displacements and political instability, will ultimately reach the borders of even the wealthiest nations. If other wealthy countries follow the Trump administration's lead and back out of financial commitments, then the needed money for adaptation may never become available.

The need for global cooperation regarding climate change geoengineering is less well-understood than the need for cooperation regarding either mitigation and adaptation. But increasingly, experts are recognizing its importance.

Wild West or International Agreement?

Geoengineering refers to large-scale technological efforts to alter the climate.

One such method, solar radiation management (SRM), involves the redirection of solar radiation back toward the sun and away from the Earth's surface using sulfates or other microscopic particles released into the atmosphere. Another SRM method is to set up giant space mirrors.

The goal of the Paris Agreement is to keep the planet from warming more than 2 degrees Celsius (on average) over the preindustrial baseline, but the agreement also aspires to keep warming to no more than 1.5°C. These are ambitious goals, especially the 1.5°C goal, given that temperatures rose 0.85°C between 1880 and 2012.

Commentators question whether, even if all the major emitters in the world aggressively pursue mitigation, global temperature increase can be held to 2°C or anything like it. If these commentators are right, some use of SRM arguably could be needed to, in effect, "buy time" for the planet during the transition to a no-carbon economy.

A basic question, therefore, is: Will the debate about, research into and (if it ever happens) deployment of SRM be a matter of the "Wild West"? That is, will it be a matter of whatever a country or even non-state actor wants to do, perhaps even partially in secret? Or will it rather be a matter of considered, transparent, inclusive decision-making by the international community as a whole?

Template for Assessing Risk

In my view, it is essential that the SRM debate take a cooperation-based path because the risks from SRM are so substantial. SRM perhaps could be effective in delaying warming effects at relatively modest out-of-pocket costs, but it could have devastating environmental consequences, including altering the weather patterns of a large part of the world.

Some potentially negative consequences cannot even be imagined at this point. SRM in theory could be weaponized and used by one nation-state to attack its enemies. Even the public discourse about SRM could be damaging. Research conducted by Kaitlin Rami, Alex Maki, Michael Vandenbergh and me suggests that overly optimistic depictions of SRM could cause public support for mitigation to plummet.

Some research into SRM and other forms of geoengineering may be sensible, but only if is done under the careful supervision of an international institution or consortium that draws on science and ethics and includes all voices in a deliberative manner.

The Paris Agreement does not explicitly address geoengineering, but it does create a template to regularly evaluate global climate risks and host ongoing negotiations and collaboration. Most notably, and for the first time in the climate change context, the Paris Agreement includes virtually all the nations of the world, including China and India.

Moreover, the agreement, while built on voluntary mitigation commitments at this point, mandates transparency in the form of national reporting. The agreement also explicitly calls for a consideration of issues of equity regarding the impacts of and responses to climate change.

And so while details are relatively few in the agreement, it represents an important first step toward governance not just for climate change mitigation, but also adaptation and potentially geoengineering.

Its generality and flexibility are its strength; as President Obama remarked, the Paris Agreement provides the "architecture" needed to address the overarching challenge of climate change. This could include the challenge of responsibly addressing the fraught question of geoengineering. Trump's withdrawal is a step backwards.

Periodical and Internet Sources Bibliography

The following articles have been selected to supplement the diverse views presented in this chapter.

Ishan Gera, "Geoengineering a Solution: Why Regulating Climate Change Using Technology Is Not a Bad Idea," *Financial Express*, January 6, 2018. http://www.financialexpress.com/lifestyle /science/geoengineering-a-solution-why-regulating-climate -change-using-technology-is-not-a-bad-idea/1003883/.

"Global Warming Solutions: Reduce Emissions," Union of Concerned Scientists. https://www.ucsusa.org/our-work/global-warming /solutions/global-warming-solutions-reduce-emissions# .WnJjkpM-fOQ.

Chelsea Gohd, "Geoengineering May Be Our Only Hope for Surviving Climate Change," Futurism, September 27, 2017. https://futurism.com/geoengineering-may-be-our-only-hope -for-surviving-climate-change/.

Nancy E. Landrum, "Geoengineering: A Dangerous Tool or Climate Control of the Future?," *Pacific Standard*, February 27, 2017. https://psmag.com/news/geoengineering-a-dangerous-tool-or -climate-control-of-the-future.

Jeff McMahon, "As Humans Fumble Climate Challenge, Interest Grows in Geoengineering," *Forbes*, September 24, 2017. https:// www.forbes.com/sites/jeffmcmahon/2017/09/24/interest -rises-in-geoengineering-as-humans-fail-to-mitigate-climate -change/#1294bcd96472.

Tim Radford, "More Harm than Good with Climate Geo- engineering," *Boulder Weekly*, December 7, 2018. http://www .boulderweekly.com/boulderganic/harm-good-climate-geo -engineering/.

Nathaniel Scharping, "If We Start Geoengineering, There's No Going Back," *Discover*, January 22, 2018. http://blogs.discovermagazine .com/d-brief/2018/01/22/geoengineering-stop-suddenly/.

Zoe Tabary, "Poor Nations Need Say in Use of Climate Geoengineering—Researchers," Reuters, November 21, 2017. https://www.reuters.com/article/climatechange-geoengineering -debate/poor-nations-need-say-in-use-of-climate -geoengineering-researchers-idUSL8N1NR4I8.

For Further Discussion

Chapter 1
1. Why is climate change a global issue?
2. What is geoengineering? Provide detailed examples

Chapter 2
1. What are the risks and benefits of CO_2 removal?
2. What are the risks and benefits of SRM?

Chapter 3
1. What are the ethical issues of geoengineering?
2. Should nations act locally or globally in the fight against climate change?

Chapter 4
1. Should wealthy nations help developing nations fight climate change?
2. Who should decide if geoengineering technology is used?

Organizations to Contact

The editors have compiled the following list of organizations concerned with the issues debated in this book. The descriptions are derived from materials provided by the organizations. All have publications or information available for interested readers. The list was compiled on the date of publication of the present volume; the information provided here may change. Be aware that many organizations take several weeks or longer to respond to inquiries, so allow as much time as possible.

Center for Climate and Energy Solutions (C2ES)
2101 Wilson Blvd., Ste. 550
Arlington, VA 22201
(703) 516-4146
email: press@C2ES.org
website: https://www.c2es.org

The C2ES is an independent, nonpartisan, nonprofit organization working to forge practical solutions to climate change. It was founded in 1998 and has become a leading source of trusted environmental science. It is one of the world's premier environmental think tanks.

Environmental Defense Fund (EDF)
1875 Connecticut Ave. NW, Ste. 600
Washington, DC 20009
(202) 387-3500
email: https://www.edf.org/contact/email/585/related/18
website: https://www.edf.org

The EDF began in the 1960s when a group of researchers connected the use of the pesticide DDT to declining falcon populations. When the county refused to stop using DDT, the group took it to court and won. In 1967 they formed a nonprofit hoping to use the courts and the financial sector to help defend the environment.

Environmental Protection Agency (EPA)

1200 Pennsylvania Ave. NW
Washington, DC 20460
(410) 305-2607
email: https://publicaccess.zendesk.com/hc/en-us/requests/new
website: https://www.epa.gov

The EPA is a federal agency created in 1970 to protect human health and the environment by writing and enforcing regulations based on laws passed by Congress. The EPA is responsible for maintaining and enforcing environmental laws in the United States. It also conducts environmental assessment, research, and education.

Greenpeace

Greenpeace Supporter Care
702 H St. NW, Ste. 300
Washington, DC 20001
(800) 722-6995
email: info@wdc.greenpeace.org
website: http://www.greenpeace.org

Greenpeace is a global independent campaigning environmental conservation organization. It uses peaceful protest to expose environmental issues around the globe. It was founded in 1971.

Sierra Club

2101 Webster St., Ste. 1300
Oakland, CA 94612
(415) 977-5500
email: information@sierraclub.org
website: https://www.sierraclub.org

Founded by conservationist John Muir in 1892, the Sierra Club is the largest grassroots environmental organization. It was influential in getting the Clean Air Act, Clean Water Act, and Endangered Species Acts passed. It is currently focusing on clean energy initiatives.

350.org
20 Jay St., Ste. 732
Brooklyn, NY 11201
(347) 460-9082
email: https://350.org/contact
website: https://350.org

350.org is a nonprofit aimed at building a global climate change movement. It was founded in 2008 by a group of university students in the United States and environmentalist Bill McKibben. Today the organization is involved in grassroots environmental activism all over the world.

Union of Concerned Scientists (UCS)
1825 K St. NW, Ste. 800
Washington, DC 20006-1232
(202) 223-6133
email: https://www.ucsusa.org/about/contact-us
website: https://www.ucsusa.org

The UCS was founded in 1969 by scientists and students at the Massachusetts Institute of Technology. They believed that science should be used to help the protect the environment rather than advance the military. The UCS hopes to combine the knowledge and influence of scientists with the passion of everyday citizens in the fight against climate change.

World Resources Institute (WRI)
10 G St. NE, Ste. 800
Washington, DC 20002
(202) 729-7600
email: delger.erdenesanaa@wri.org
website: http://www.wri.org

The World Resources Institute was created in 1982 to advocate for the needs of humans and nature alike. It carries out rigorous policy research in the hopes of finding the best solutions to climate change. The organization also strives to help build sustainable cities.

World Wildlife Fund (WWF)
1250 Twenty-Fourth St. NW
Washington, DC 20037
(800) 960-0993
email: membership@wwfus.org
website: www.worldwildlife.org

The WWF is an international nonprofit dedicated to preserving nature. It strives to find the best ways for humans and nature to coexist. While it is most known for its animal conservation efforts, the WWF also works to prevent climate change for the survival of all life on Earth.

Yale Program on Climate Change Communication
Yale School of Forestry & Environmental Studies
195 Prospect St.
New Haven, CT 06511
(203) 432-5100
email: climatechange@yale.edu
website: http://climatecommunication.yale.edu

Education is an important tool in the fight against climate change. The Yale Program on Climate Change Communication is researching the most effective ways to educate the public about climate change. It conducts scientific studies on public opinion and behavior.

Bibliography of Books

Michael Anderson, *Global Warming*. New York, NY: Britannica Educational Publishing in Association with Rosen Educational Services, 2012.

Jeffrey Bennett, *A Global Warming Primer: Answering Your Questions About the Science, the Consequences, and the Solutions*. Boulder, CO: Big Kid Science, 2017.

Rachel Carson, *Silent Spring*. New York, NY: Houghton Mifflin, 1962.

L. H. Colligan, *Global Warming*. New York, NY: Marshall Cavendish Benchmark, 2012.

Jeff Goodell, *The Water Will Come: Rising Seas, Sinking Cities, and the Remaking of the Civilized World*. New York, NY: Little, Brown, 2017.

David M. Haugen, *Global Warming* (Opposing Viewpoints). New York, NY: Greenhaven, 2010.

Bridget Heos, *It's Getting Hot in Here: The Past, Present, and Future of Climate Change*. New York, NY: Houghton Mifflin, 2015.

Debra Miller, *Global Warming*. Detroit, MI: Greenhaven, 2013.

Oliver Morton, *The Planet Remade: How Geoengineering Could Change the World*. Princeton, NJ: Princeton University Press, 2017.

John Rafferty, *Climate and Climate Change*. New York, NY: Brittanica, 2011.

Jack Stilgoe, *Experiment Earth: Responsible Innovation in Geoengineering*. New York, NY: Routledge, 2016.

Jennifer Swanson, *Geoengineering Earth's Climate: Resetting the Thermostat*. Minneapolis, MN: Twenty-First Century Books, 2017.

Shelley Tanaka, *Climate Change.* Berkeley CA: Groundwood, 2012.

Sally M. Walker, *We Are the Weather Makers: The History of Climate Change.* Somerville, MA: Candlewick, 2009.

John Woodward, *Climate Change.* New York, NY: DK Publishing, 2013.

Mitsutsune Yamaguchi, ed., *Climate Change Mitigation: A Balanced Approach to Climate Change.* New York, NY: Springer, 2014.

Index